Kenya: Identity of A Nation

Godfrey Mwakikagile

Kenya: Identity of A Nation
Godfrey Mwakikagile

First Edition

ISBN 978-0-9802587-9-0

New Africa Press
Pretoria, South Africa

Dedication

To the youth of Africa
in whose hands lies the future
of our continent

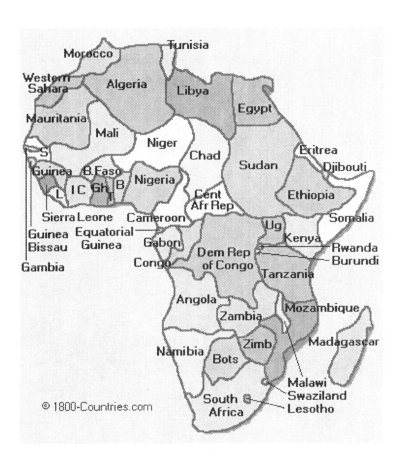

Contents

Acknowledgements

Introduction

Chapter One:
Kenya: An Overview

Chapter Two:
The Decade Before Independence

Chapter Three:
A Few Years After Independence

Chapter Four:
Kenyan Provinces

Chapter Five:
The People of Kenya: An Ethnic Profile

Chapter Six:
The Traditional Way of Life:
A Look at African Cultures

Chapter Seven:
Ethnic Conflicts in Kenya: A Nation Divided

Chapter Eight:
Kenya in Contemporary Times

Chapter Nine:
Kenya's National Character

Appendix I:

Race and Culture: A Luo Perspective

Appendix II:

The Indians of East Africa

Appendix III:

The Swahili People and The Swahili Culture

Acknowledgements

THIS work drew its inspiration from the people of Kenya who, as a nation, are the main focus of my study.

I wish to express my profound gratitude to them in full acknowledgement of the fact that without them, I would not have written this book.

I am also grateful to the sources I have used to document my work.

I also owe a debt of gratitude to the individuals and institutions whose material I have used in the appendix to shed more light on the focus of this study.

It is customary for writers to name in their acknowledgements the people who have contributed to the success of their works while claiming responsibility for the mistakes which may be found in their writings.

Much as I would like to do the same thing, I have decided not to name any individuals not only because space does not allow me to do so to convey the depth of my gratitude to them individually; I have not done so also because I don't want to do injustice to any of them by inadvertently omitting their names from the list.

My work may be flawed in conception and may be even in execution, but it is none of their fault, and their contribution to the successful completion of my work is evident throughout the book. And I bear full responsibility for any mistakes which may be found in this study.

We are mere mortals, with frailties, and should realise that when we scan the horizon, we are able to see far only because we stand on the shoulders of others. No individual can claim credit for cumulative knowledge of human experience.

But I must also state that my background as an East African from Tanzania proved to be an invaluable asset - in terms of my knowledge of the region - when I undertook this study focusing on Kenya, our neighbour, and fellow member of the East African Community (EAC) comprising five countries - Kenya, Uganda, Tanzania, Rwanda, and Burundi - which we hope one day will unite under one federal government.

Only time will tell.

Introduction

This book is about Kenya as a country and as a nation. It is also a work of comparative analysis in the African context. It also focuses on the nation as an entity with its own personality and national character.

Kenya is one of the most well-known countries in Africa for several reasons. It is one of the major tourist destinations in the world. It is, by African standards, one of the most developed countries on the continent. It also occupies a special place in the history of Africa because of the role it played in the struggle for independence.

It was in Kenya where Mau Mau, a mass uprising on an unprecedented scale against colonial injustices, was fought. Mau Mau was one of the bloodiest and most successful wars in colonial history, and it thrust Kenya into the international spotlight.

It also earned the Mau Mau freedom fighters distinction as some of the most outstanding champions of freedom for Africans and as some of the most revered fighters in the struggle for African liberation from imperial rule. They are still remembered today not only as gallant fighters but as some of the most inspiring pioneers of the African independence movement.

Jomo Kenyatta himself, who was accused of leading Mau Mau and who later became the first president of Kenya, was one of the most respected African leaders and was revered across the continent as the Grand Old Man of the African independence movement. Also cordially known as "The Burning Spear," he cast a long shadow over Kenya and the rest of the continent and his formidable personality and legendary role as the leader of the independence movement also played a major role in thrusting his country on the international scene.

Kenya is also the economic powerhouse of East Africa. It has the most developed and the strongest economy among all the countries which constitute the East African Community (EAC). They are Kenya, Uganda, Tanzania, Rwanda, and Burundi. It is, in fact, the most developed country in the entire region of Eastern Africa which includes the countries in the Horn of Africa: Somalia, Ethiopia, Eritrea, and Djibouti.

This work is a general introduction to Kenya as a country and as a nation. Subjects covered include a short history of the country, its geography including administrative provinces and various ethnic groups in those provinces; Mau Mau and the struggle for independence; the early years of independence; political developments through the decades; the cultures of different ethnic groups; the country's natural resources and much more.

Also addressed in the book is the country's ethnic diversity and the impact it has had on Kenya's stability as a country and as a nation composed of different ethnic and racial groups.

The work also looks at Kenya's national character from my background as an East African myself from neighbouring Tanzania in a study of comparative analysis between Kenya and Tanzania as political entities with different national characters to demonstrate that nations do, indeed, have different national characters.

Chapter One:

Kenya: An Overview

KENYA is one of the most well-known countries in Africa. It is also one of the most prosperous, although it does not have an abundance of natural resources like neighbouring Tanzania.

It is bordered by Uganda on the West, Sudan on the northwest, Ethiopia on the north and northeast, Somalia on the east, and by Tanzania on the south.

Although the country's economy depends largely on agriculture, only about 12 per cent of the land is suitable for cultivation. Six per cent is used for grazing.

Like all the countries on the continent, Kenya is primarily an agricultural country with only a few major cities and towns. They are Nairobi, the capital; Mombasa, the country's main port and outlet to the sea; Kisumu; and Nakuru, the capital of the Rift Valley Province in west-central Kenya which was founded in the early 20th century as a centre of European settlement.

Nakuru is Kenya's fourth largest city and a growing commercial and industrial centre whose manufactures include textiles, processed foods and pyrethrum extract. Nearby is Lake Nakuru, a small soda water lake. The surrounding area has been developed as a national park known for its flamingo haunts.

The third largest city, after Nairobi and Mombasa, is Kisumu which is also the capital of Nyanza Province in southwestern Kenya. It is located on Kavirondo Gulf, an arm of Lake Victoria, and is the principal lake port of Kenya. It is also the commercial centre of a prosperous farm region. Its manufactures include refined sugar, frozen fish, textiles, beer, and processed sisal. An ethanol plant was built in the 1980s.

Kisumu, formerly known as Port Florence, is also a major tourist centre with attractions of Lake Victoria and nearby wildlife. The railway from Mombasa reached Kisumu in 1901 and was one of the major engineering achievements in the history of colonial Africa.

The other major towns of Kenya are Thika, Machakos, Eldoret, and Naivasha.

Kenya also has a number of universities, including the University of Nairobi, Jomo Kenyatta University of Science and Technology, Egerton University, and Moi University.

The vast majority of Kenyans are engaged in farming, largely of the subsistence type. Coffee, tea, maize, wheat and pyrethrum are grown in the highlands, mainly on small African-owned farms; while coconuts, pineapples, cashew nuts, cotton, sugar cane and sisal are grown in low-lying areas including the coastal region.

Kenya's major exports are coffee, tea, fruits, vegetables and flowers. About 75 per cent of the people depend on agriculture.

Much of the country is savanna where large numbers of cattle are pastured. Kenya also produces significant quantities of dairy goods, pork, poultry, and eggs.

The country's leading manufactures include consumer goods such as textiles, plastics, furniture, cigarettes, leather goods, refined petroleum, processed food, cement, and metal products. The country's chief minerals are limestone, soda ash, gold, salt, flouspar, and titanium.

The country straddles the equator and has four main regions: the narrow fertile coastal strip with rain forests and mangrove swamps; the vast dry scrub-land pastures crossed by the country's main rivers, the Tana and the Athi; the highlands, cut by the Great Rift Valley, where Mount Kenya and Mount Elgon stand and where the rich volcanic soil, moderate temperatures and ample rainfall sustain most farm crops; and the western (Nyanza) plateau stretching to Lake Victoria, which is an area of farmlands, forests and grasslands.

About 98 per cent of the population is black African, mostly of Bantu stock, comprising 42 major ethnic groups or tribes. The biggest are the Kikuyu, the Luhya, the Luo, the Kamba, the Kisii, and the Meru.

There are also Indian, Arab and European communities who constitute about 2 per cent of the population.

A disproportionately large number of people live in the southwest, mainly in the fertile highlands where Nairobi, the capital and largest city, is located.

The majority of Kenyans are Christian. But there is a significant number of Muslims mainly in the coastal area. Many Kenyans are also followers of traditional religions and practise their faiths the same way their ancestors did before the introduction of Christianity and Islam.

Besides agriculture, the other important sectors of the economy are manufacturing, mainly involving processing farm products, production of consumer goods including import-substitution items, and oil refining; forestry and lumbering; and mining, although the country does not have a lot minerals. Kenya's agricultural sector is also known for its livestock and dairy products including poultry.

Kenya is known worldwide for its national parks and game reserves. And, together with neighbouring Tanzania, it is one of the biggest tourist destinations in the world.

Its major attractions include the Great Rift Valley -

Lake Turkana, once known as Lake Rudolph, and the country's largest lake, is located in this valley.

Other major attractions are Mount Kenya; Tsavo National Park which was made famous by its man-eating lions during the construction of the Kenya-Uganda Railway starting from Mombasa; Nairobi, Aberdare and Lake Nakuru national parks; Masai Mara, Amboseli and Samburu game reserves; and the Nairobi national museum.

The tourism industry is the biggest foreign exchange earner. Hundreds of thousands of tourists visit Kenya every year. The nation's leading tourist attractions are the national park sanctuaries for lions, elephants, leopards, giraffes, zebras, gazelles and other wild animals.

The area which came to be known as Kenya has a long history. Together with Tanzania and Ethiopia, it is considered to be the cradle of mankind. The three East African countries collectively constitute the scientists' Garden of Eden.

Some of its earliest contacts with the outside world were between the coastal tribes and the Arabs from the Arabian peninsula. Trade between the two regions was brisk by 100 A.D. Arabs built settlements along the coast and built city-states including Mombasa, Malindi and Pate. And throughout the Middle Ages, the region also attracted traders from India and other parts of Asia including the Middle East.

The Portuguese were the first Europeans to arrive in the region. They arrived in 1498 and established trading posts along the coast. They controlled much of it but their dominance ended when they were driven out by the Arabs in 1729. From 1740 Arabs ruled the Kenyan coast from Zanzibar which was the capital of the Sultanate dominating the East African coast.

The coast remained under Arab control until 1887 when the British East Africa Company leased the Kenyan coast from the sultan of Zanzibar. Kenya became a British protectorate in 1895, and a crown colony in 1920.

The British opened the interior with imported Indian labour and encouraged European settlement. It was these Indians who mostly built the Kenya-Uganda Railway (1895 – 1901) from Mombasa to Kisumu on the shores of Lake Victoria in order to facilitate trade with the interior and with Uganda, and consolidate imperial rule.

In 1903 the first settlers, mostly British including members of the aristocracy, established themselves as large-scale farmers in the highlands of central Kenya by taking land from the indigenous Kikuyu, the Embu, the Maasai and others. It was also during the same period that Indian merchants moved inland from the coast.

From the 1920s to the 1940s, white settlers not only controlled the government but owned extensive farmlands to the detriment of the indigenous people. And while Indians owned small businesses especially shops in towns and also worked in the government as lower-level employees, Africans worked mostly on farms as subsistence farmers and grew coffee and cotton on a small scale. Africans also worked as low-paid labourers in towns especially in Nairobi, the capital.

In the 1920s, Africans began to protest against racial injustice and their inferior status in the hierarchy of the races established by the white settlers. Political awakening among Africans, fuelled by expropriation of their land especially in the central highlands occupied by the Kikuyu, led to demands for justice from the colonial rulers. But their demands were ignored.

In 1928, Jomo Kenyatta who was secretary of a Kikuyu political association began campaigning for land reform and political rights for Africans. His campaign was also ignored. The result was Mau Mau, one of the bloodiest uprisings in colonial history.

Casualty figures vary. Estimates of Africans killed range from 20,000 to 100,000, and even up to 300,000. Only a few whites, not more than 150, were killed by the

Mau Mau fighters.

Demographer John Blacker, in his article *The Demography of Mau Mau* published in *African Affairs* in 2007, says about 50,000 Africans were killed during Mau Mau, half of whom were children under 10.

By the time the Emergency came to an end in 1960, at least 1,000 Mau Mau fighters and sympathisers had been hanged.

Many of them were hanged for simply possessing an "illegal" firearm or for other offences less than murder and for which capital punishment could not be justified.

Kenyatta was accused of leading Mau Mau and was sentenced to seven years' imprisonment. He was released from prison in July 1961 and placed in detention in Gatundu near Nairobi until August 21st when all restrictions imposed on him were lifted. Mau Mau lasted until 1960.

On 12 December 1963, Kenya won independence from Britain and Kenyatta became prime minister. Exactly one year later, Kenya became a republic and Kenyatta its first president.

The Kenya African National Union (KANU) which spearheaded the struggle for independence under Kenyatta's leadership was the dominant political party. But its dominance was challenged shortly after independence when Vice President Jaramogi Oginga Odinga broke with Kenyatta and formed an opposition party in March 1966. The party was named the Kenya People's Union (KPU) and proclaimed that Kenya was not yet free.

But it did not last long. On 27 October 1966, Odinga was put under house arrest after an anti-government demonstration by the KPU. Three days later, the KPU was banned, leaving KANU the only legal political party in the country.

Less than two years later, the government began a campaign in March 1968 to "Africanise" the country. In the next six years, thousands of Asian shopkeepers, mostly

Indians and Pakistanis, were forced to leave the country. The majority had British passports and were therefore British citizens.

But many Kenyans of Asian origin were also forced to leave because of the hostile political climate, although it did not reach the level of virulence it did in neighbouring Uganda where only a few years later Idi Amin expelled Asians from the country in 1972. Ugandan citizens of Asian origin were also kicked out.

Although a significant number of Asians left Kenya because of political conditions as a result of "Africanisation," many others left voluntarily. So did Europeans who numbered about 55,000 in 1962, the year before independence.

When Kenya won independence, it was the most developed country in East Africa in terms of infrastructural development, commerce, health facilities and other areas. And it still is today.

Although Kenya has enjoyed relative peace and stability since independence, it has also faced a number of political crises through the years including ethnic cleavages between the country's largest ethnic groups, especially the Kikuyu and the Luo. And in the seventies, it had to contend with Idi Amin's unpredictable behaviour when the Ugandan dictator threatened the country.

In July 1976, Amin threatened to bomb Kenya. His threats were in response to what the Kenyan government had done to Uganda, according to Amin. Kenyatta's government had allowed Israel's planes to land for refuelling after the daring raid on Uganda on 4 July 1976 to rescue hostages held by Arab hijackers. The Kenyan government asked its citizens to leave Uganda as the two countries came to the brink of war. But Idi Amin calmed down and friendly relations were re-established in August the same year.

There was also tension between the two countries because of a territorial dispute and Amin's claim that

Kenya's western province was part of Uganda.

Kenya also faced an uncertain future during that period because of Kenyatta's age. He was in his eighties and concern arose in the 1970s as to what would happen to the country after he died.

When politicians attempted to hold public meetings on the subject of a successor for Kenyatta, they were warned by the attorney general, Charles Njonjo, in October 1976 that it was a crime punishable by death even to imagine Kenyatta's death.

It was also during the same period that Tanzania closed its border with Kenya. The border was closed in February 1977 following a dispute over the shutting down of an airline – the East African Airways (EAA) – that had been jointly owned and operated by Kenya, Uganda and Tanzania. Kenyan officials said it was an effort by Tanzanian leaders to prevent the people of socialist Tanzania from coming to Kenya to see the economic prosperity enjoyed by Kenyans under free enterprise.

About 10 years later, Tanzania abandoned socialism following the collapse of the Soviet Union which marked the end of communism and socialist regimes around the world.

The closing of the border also had to with a dispute Tanzania had with Kenya because the Kenyan government allowed many supporters of Idi Amin to live in Kenya after Tanzania kicked Amin out of Uganda in April 1979. There was no chance then that Tanzania would re-open the border.

Kenya also had a border dispute with Somalia in the sixties involving the Northern Frontier District, now known as Northeastern Province, which was claimed by Somalia. The Somali constitute the dominant ethnic group in this province.

The dispute led to sporadic fighting between the two sides from 1963 to 1968, and the matter has not been entirely resolved. Many Somalis on both sides of the border want the region to be part of Greater Somalia.

Kenya has always been a tourist haven, attracting visitors and hunters from different parts of the world for decades, even as far back as the 1930s. And the seventies witnessed one of the major changes by the Kenyan government in the tourism sector. In an effort to preserve the country's wildlife, the government announced in May 1977 a ban on the killing of elephants, rhinoceroses, leopards, zebras, and other wild animals.

The move was applauded by conservationists in Kenya and other countries but was deplored by Kenya's 300 or more professional hunters who were told to convert hunting trips for tourists into photographic safaris. Unfortunately, the ban did not stop poaching despite government attempts to do so.

The seventies also witnessed a major transition in Kenya's national life when President Jomo Kenyatta died in his sleep on 22 August 1978. He was believed to be about 89 but had no record of his birth. What is known is that he was born before Kenya was colonised and lived long enough to rule Kenya himself after winning the struggle for independence.

His death was a milestone in Kenya's history and hundreds of thousands of Kenyans lined the route of his funeral procession. Daniel arap Moi, who had served as vice president under Kenyatta, became president without opposition.

A former school headmaster, President Moi made one of his first decrees the abolition of school fees. He also ordered free milk served at schools and promised to increase the number of teachers and other school personnel. And to emphasise his claim that he strongly believed in human rights, he released all 16 political prisoners who had been imprisoned by Kenyatta. Yet he himself went on to rule Kenya with an iron fist, sometimes surpassing Kenyatta in political repression and did not relinquish power until more than two decades later.

Kenya officially became a one-party state in June 1982 when parliament unanimously approved the ruling Kenya African National Union (KANU) as the only legal party.

In August 1982, an attempt was made to overthrow the government but it was suppressed. About 145 persons were killed. Also, many people were wounded. Kenya's 2,100 air force was disbanded and those suspected of taking part in the abortive coup were imprisoned. Universities were also closed because of student support for the coup attempt.

Throughout the 1980s, President Moi consolidated his position and rejected demands for democratisation. He continued to maintain a tight lid on the opposition and conducted periodic purges of his government to weed out suspected opponents. The economy also deteriorated under his rule.

In 1988, riots erupted in Nairobi and other parts of the country after a number of his political opponents who were demanding democracy were arrested. Their arrest led to increased opposition and criticism of his government in other countries, forcing him to legalise multi-party democracy.

Moi stayed in office until 2002 when he could no longer run for office because of a constitutional amendment which prevented him from doing so. He was succeed by his former vice president, Mwai Kibaki, who was the leader of the biggest opposition party, the National Rainbow Coalition (NARC), which ended 40 years of political dominance by KANU.

In 2004, an issue which may partly determine the future of Kenya in terms of race relations and political stability got national attention when a number of people from the Maasai tribe began to protest over land which they said was unjustly taken away from them by the British colonial rulers. They said the lease signed 99 years ago by the British had expired.

There were rumblings from other groups in Kenya who

felt that they also had been dispossessed of their land by the British colonial rulers. The long-term leases, some more than 900 years long, had been forced on them by the British without the slightest concern for the well-being of the indigenous people.

The land question has bedeviled other African countries which have a significant number of people of European descent who acquired land at the expense of the indigenous people. And it continues to be one of the most contentious issues in race relations in those countries especially in southern Africa. Zimbabwe is a prime example.

Chapter Two:

The Decade Before Independence

THE decade before independence was dominated by the campaign for freedom more than anything else. And one of the most important events in this nationalist campaign was the Mau Mau insurgency.

The quest for freedom was a two-pronged attack on colonial rule. It was pursued along constitutional lines, with leaders like Oginga Odinga and Tom Mboya (when Jomo Kenyatta was in prison) addressing mass rallies demanding independence; and on the battle field in a low-intensity guerrilla warfare waged by the Mau Mau freedom fighters to compel the British to relinquish control of the country in order for Africans to rule themselves.

The conditions were intolerable for Africans, especially the Kikuyu. As George Padmore, a political activist and Pan-Africanist from Trinidad who knew and worked closely with Jomo Kenyatta and Kwame Nkrumah in Britain in the 1940s, and who later became adviser to Prime Minister and thereafter President Nkrumah, stated in his book first published in 1956, *Pan-Africanism or Communism? The Coming Struggle for Africa*:

Although the name has never been satisfactorily defined, as no such word as 'Mau Mau' exists in the Kikuyu language, its socio-economic causes are easier to explain.

Mau Mau is not an organized political movement with a regular membership, officers and constitution like the Kenya African Union. It is a spontaneous revolt of a declassed section of the African rural population, uprooted from its tribal lands and driven into urban slum life without any hope of gainful employment....

All the pseudo-anthropological assertions about Mau Mau being a 'religion,' is sheer nonsense. Mau Mau hymn singing and oath taking are merely psychological devices borrowed by desperate young men from freemasonry and missionary sources to bind their adherents to their cause.

In trying to elevate Mau Mau into a 'religion' and ascribing obscene practices to them, the whites hope to shift all responsibility for what has happened upon the Africans and explain it all away as a sudden reversion to savagery, which demands their continued presence in Kenya to bring the Africans back on the path to civilization....

Like the slave revolts of Ancient Rome, the supporters of Mau Mau are fighting for land, without which they prefer death. - (George Padmore, *Pan-Africanism or Communism? The Coming Struggle for Africa* (London: Dennis Dobson, 1956), pp. 247, and 248).

The Kikuyu were joined by the Embu and the Meru, whose land had also been taken away by the white settlers although on a smaller scale, and the uprising had the potential to spread to other parts of Kenya which had white settlements.

Yet, all the Africans in Kenya shared basically the same grievances the Kikuyu and other people in the Central Province had towards the colonial rulers. They were all victims of colonial injustices which were racial and racist in character.

From 1945, following the end of World War II and just five years before the beginning of the pivotal decade, the fifties, Africans petitioned the colonial government in Kenya and the Colonial Office in London, making it clear that they wanted their grievances to be addressed by the

25

colonial rulers. They were ignored.

The campaign was led by Jomo Kenyatta who was the leader of the Kenya African Union (KAU), a party which had support among the people of different tribes across the country.

Compounding the problem was the demand by the British settlers themselves for the establishment of a white nation, and for independence under white minority rule. They saw Kenya as another South Africa, Australia or New Zealand where white settlers established independent states, excluding the indigenous people from the government.

Because of the intransigence of the colonial authorities, many Africans felt that an armed struggle was the only option they had left to try and compel the British settlers to relinquish power in what was predominantly a black African country.

In 1946, a Kikuyu group known as Anake a Forty (warriors of 1940) articulated its position forcefully, stating explicitly that only war against the white settlers would enable the Kikuyu and other Africans to regain their land.

They appealed to their compatriots – of all tribes – to fight for their rights by any means available to them, including the use of violence.

By 1948, 1.25 million Kikuyus were confined to only 2,000 square miles. The area to which they were restricted was not only small; it was also unsuitable for agriculture. By remarkable contrast, 30,000 white settlers occupied 12,000 square miles and almost all the best agricultural land was under their ownership.

To make things worse, tens of thousands of Kikuyus, no fewer than 120,000, became tenant farmers on white-owned land where they were allowed to farm on small plots in exchange for their labour. And this was the land that had been takes away from them by whites. Now they found themselves to be strangers, and virtual slaves for

26

whites, on their own land.

And between 1938 and 1946, whites demanded even more days of labour from the Kikuyu and imposed further restrictions on them, denying them access to land they had previously been able to use.

The year 1947 was a turning point in this struggle, for, it was then that many members of the Kikuyu, Embu, Meru and Kamba tribes began administering and taking oaths, swearing that they were ready to fight and die for their rights as Africans who had been dispossessed of their land and subjected to other injustices by the white settlers who lived at their expense.

In fact, by 1953, almost half of all the Kikuyus had no land rights at all. Deprived of land, they sank deeper into poverty, faced starvation and other problems including unemployment, and overpopulation in areas to which they were restricted.

The colonial authorities made things even worse when earlier in 1947 police shot and killed three Africans during a strike by African workers at Uplands Bacon Factory; an attack Africans saw as a flagrant violation of their rights including the sanctity of life the colonial rulers felt they were not bound to respect as long as lives lost were African, not white.

All that contributed to the birth of Mau Mau. As an organisation of disgruntled Africans bound by common suffering, Mau Mau is believed to have been started in 1950.

In 1951, the Kenya African Union – which later evolved into KANU and led Kenya to independence – sent a delegation to London to present its demands on behalf of Africans in Kenya but its demands were rejected by the British government.

It was obvious that all avenues towards peaceful resolution of the crisis were closed. And the crisis had reached boiling point.

In August 1951, people including government officials

started hearing reports that secret meetings were being held in the forests, including the Aberdares, by Kikuyus and that they were taking oaths to kick out the white man and regain their land.

Before then in the late 1940s, the leaders of the banned Kenya Central Association (KCA), once led by Harry Thuku, began planning a campaign of civil obedience in which all Kikuyus would be urged to participate to protest land expropriation by whites. Those who agreed to participate vowed to take oaths, a common practice among the Kikuyu and the other tribes, the Embu and the Meru, also involved in this conflict with whites.

The oath rituals were for civil disobedience but later became much more serious, requiring participants to fight whites who had taken the land away from them.

The seeds had been planted. And it was from all this that Mau Mau finally emerged and became a potent force in the fifties during the struggle for independence as a military expression of political and economic aspirations of dispossessed Africans, one of the most successful uprisings in the history of colonial Africa.

Initially, the members of this secret organisation were almost exclusively Kikuyus but later embraced the Embu and the Meru who are also closely related to the Kikuyu; the Kikuyu's real name, in their own language, is Gikuyu. But they are popularly known as Kikuyu.

Besides these three related tribes, the Kamba and Maasai also joined the revolt although on a smaller scale. But their involvement showed that the uprising had spread beyond the White Highlands and involved other Africans, most of whom sympathised with the plight of the Kikuyu as well as the Embu and the Meru as victims of colonial injustices which also affected them, only in varying degrees especially in terms of land ownership and expropriation.

In August 1952, the colonial government imposed a curfew on three areas around Nairobi where some people, believed to be members of Mau Mau, burned down some houses belonging to Africans – mostly Kikuyu – who refused to take an oath to join Mau Mau.

In October 1952, Senior Chief Waruhiu was killed in broad daylight. He was speared to death on a main road on the outskirts of Nairobi. He had recently spoken out against Mau Mau and criticised those who were opposed to the government. He was a known supporter of the British colonial rulers and settlers and was hated by many of his own people, fellow Kikuyus, and other Africans who saw him as a traitor.

The new governor of Kenya, Sir Evelyn Baring, had a swift response to the killing of an African sympathiser of colonial rule and to reports that the Kikiyu and their compatriots were attacking whites on their farms. He declared a state of emergency on 20 October 1952. The declaration of a state of emergency also amounted to a declaration of war on Mau Mau by the colonial government.

Just the day before, on October 19th, the British government announced that it was sending troops to Kenya to fight Mau Mau. And soon thereafter, Kenyatta and his colleagues were arrested, thus virtually decapitating the Kenya African Union (KAU) – but it was not defeated:

At dawn on October 21st, 1952, Jomo Kenyatta, the president (of KAU), and twenty-five other officers were arrested. From then on, mass arrests of members of the Union have taken place daily during the past four years. - (George Padmore, *Pan-Africanism or Communism*, ibid., p. 249).

Others arrested included Achieng Oneko, KAU's secretary-general; Fred Kubai, chairman of the Nairobi branch; Bildad Kaggia, secretary of the Nairobi branch; Kung'u Karumba. and Paul Ngei. They were all leaders of national stature and were charged with leading Mau Mau which was banned in 1950.

Altogether, about 100 leaders were arrested on the same day. And up to 8,000 people were rounded up and detained during the first 25 days of the Emergency. Also, many white settlers took the law into their own hands to deal with suspected Mau Mau fighters and sympathisers, imposing harsh and cruel punishment on them.

The trial of Jomo Kenyatta and his compatriots lasted 59 days and was the longest and most sensational in British colonial history. They were all convicted and sentenced to seven years' imprisonment with hard labour. They were sent to prison at Kapenguria in an arid region in northern Kenya.

Just the day after the trial ended and the sentence was given on 8 April 1953, the Kenyan colonial government placed under police protection the magistrate who had presided over the trial and delivered the judgment. His name was Thacker, and he was flown out of the country and given "asylum" in England.

Although KAU leaders were now in prison, the colonial government still allowed the African political organisation to exist, but not for long. On 8 June 1953, Governor Baring issued a statement, which was read by Chief Native Commissioner E. H. Windley in a radio broadcast, declaring:

There is no doubt that there are members of the Kenya African Union who have no connection with violent movements; but action has been taken because the Government has satisfied itself that there is ample evidence to show that the Kenya African Union has often been used as a cover by the Mau Mau terrorist organization, and that, both before and after the emergency was declared, there has been connection between many members of the Kenya African Union and Mau Mau terrorists. - (Quoted, ibid., p. 253).

Yet, there was no evidence linking Kenyatta and many of his colleagues to Mau Mau.

The war against Mau Mau was the biggest colonial war in Africa since the Boer War. More 30,000 British troops were involved, together with the local police force, the Kenya Regiment which recruited exclusively from among the European male population, the Kikuyu Home Guards, and the King's African Rifles (KAR) which was Kenya's national army.

Africans called Mau Mau, the Kikuyu Land Liberation Army or the Land and Freedom Armies, and saw it as the appropriate response to racial injustices being perpetrated against them by the white settlers.

The forces fighting Mau Mau were reinforced by soldiers of the King's African Rifles from neighbouring Uganda and Tanganyika, both of which were also British colonies like Kenya. A total of 55,000 troops were involved during the course of the conflict. But they did not exceed 10,000 at any one time during the operation against Mau Mau.

Colonel Ewart Grogan, a member of the Kenya Legislative Council who had immigrated to Kenya from South Africa and who was the doyen of the settler community in Kenya, had this to say about the whole situation:

We Europeans have to go on ruling this country and rule it with iron discipline....Teach the whole Kikuyu tribe a lesson by providing a 'psychic shock'....If the whole of the Kikuyu land unit is reverted to the Crown, then every Kikuyu would know that our little queen was a great Bwana. - (Ewart Grogan, quoted by George Padmore, *Pan-African or Communism?*, pp. 255, and 256).

When the Kenya African Union (KAU) was banned in 1953 – so were all the other African national political parties – it was clear to many Africans that Mau Mau was the only answer to their problems with the white settlers. Fighting escalated soon after the parties were banned, and more people joined Mau Mau.

Most of the fighting took place in the Central Province, the Aberdares (Nyandarua), around Mount Kenya, and in Nakuru District. The main and most well-known leader of the Mau Mau fighters was Dedan Kimathi.

There were two others: Waruhiu Itote, also known as General China, who was the leader the Mau Mau in the forests around Mount Kenya, and Stanley Mathenge. Kimathi led the Mau Mau in the Aberdare forest.

Kimathi was finally captured by the Kikuyu Tribal Police on 21 October 1956 in Nyeri. They were led by one of the colonial police officers, Ian Henderson.

Henderson even wrote a book about his exploits, *The Hunt for Kimathi* published in 1958, and became a hero to the white settlers. But soon after Kenya won independence, he was deported. He was highly notorious for his brutal tactics and for torturing Mau Mau suspects and sympathisers.

Dedan Kimathi was hanged in Nyeri on 17 February 1957 and his execution marked the beginning of the end of the Mau Mau uprising.

The Emergency lasted until January 1960 but some Mau Mau fighters remained in the forest until 1963, the year Kenya won independence.

It was a bitter and protracted conflict. Whites were attacked on their farms; also government buildings and police stations were attacked by the Mau Mau fighters. Africans, including chiefs and headmen, who were seen as sympathisers of the colonial rulers were also targeted. Many of them were killed.

Most of the fighting took place in the forests which was the main sanctuary and stronghold for Mau Mau and where British soldiers and their African troops went in search of the fighters.

As the fighting went on, the colonial government took draconian measures to try and disrupt Mau Mau by forcing tens of thousands of Kikuyus into concentration camps including villages which were euphemistically called – by the authorities – "protected" villages; nothing but a form of prison.

These villages were in the Kikuyu reserves which were

the main concentration camps into which the Kikuyu had been forced in a desperate attempt by the colonial authorities to contain and neutralise Mau Mau.

By 1955, the British had gained the upper hand in their war against Mau Mau. And by October that year, more than 1.5 million Kikuyus had been placed in concentration camps, so-called protected villages. Altogether, there were 854 such "villages" for that large number of people. And life was hell in those camps.

The British saw themselves winning the war. But even with their superior weapons including the Royal Air Force dropping bombs on Mau Mau hideouts in the Aberdares and elsewhere, the fighting continued.

The Mau Mau fighters were not defeated. They refused to surrender.

Government forces were led by General Sir George Erskine, former commander of the British army in the Suez Canal Zone in Egypt. He was assisted by Major-General W.R.N. Hinde who served as director of operations.

On 20 October 1963, to mark the first anniversary of the declaration of emergency, Governor Evelyn Baring announced that there was an imperative need to expand the armed forces and intensify the military campaign against Mau Mau.

Ironically, it was a view that was not shared by the commanding officer. On the day after the governor announced the new measures, General Erskine, in what amounted to a prophetic statement, said there was no military solution to the problems of Kenya. And went to say:

(The problem was) purely political – how Europeans, Africans and Asians can live in harmony on a long-term basis. If the people of Kenya could address themselves to this problem and find a solution they would have achieved far more than I could do with security forces. - (General George Erskine, quoted by George Padmore, *Pan-African or Communism?*, p. 257).

The British knew this was a war of attrition which they could probably not win outright and, by 1959, they started making some concessions to Africans, including land ownership in many areas and whose denial was at the core of the conflict.

And on the political front, African leaders stepped up their campaign for independence. The most prominent during that period were Jaramogi Oginga Odinga and Tom Mboya, coincidentally, both members of what then - and for many years thereafter - the second-largest ethnic group in Kenya, the Luo, next to the Kikuyu who constituted the biggest fighting force of Mau Mau.

In the absence of KAU as a legal political party for Africans, Mboya formed the National People's Convention Party (NPCP) in 1957 and was elected a member of the Legislative Council (Legco), which was the national legislature for the colony. The Legislative Council was "evenly" divided. It had 14 Africans representing the entire African population of 6 million, and 14 members representing 60,000 whites.

Mboya worked with other Africans in Legco and elsewhere to demand equal representation in the colonial legislature and to campaign for independence.

When the colonial government eased its restrictions on political activities by Africans, Mboya and other African leaders revived the Kenya African Union (KAU) and transformed it into the Kenya African National Union (KANU) in May 1960. He was elected KANU's secretary-general.

James Gichuru, a Kikuyu, was elected KANU's president and held that post until after Kenyatta was freed. Gichuru became one of the first cabinet members in Kenyatta's government soon after independence.

KANU was essentially a union of KAU, NPCP led by Mboya, and the Kenya Independence Movement (KIM) led by Dr. Gikonyo Kiano, a Kikuyu, who also became a cabinet member under Kenyatta after Kenya won independence.

Oginga Odinga – who could have become the first president of Kenya – was Kenya's most prominent leader, besides Tom Mboya, when Kenyatta was in prison. After Kenyatta was released from prison, Odinga stepped aside and let Kenyatta take over the leadership of the party which finally led the country to independence on 12 December 1963.

Kenyatta became Kenya's first prime minister, then president one year after independence. Oginga Odinga served as vice president, and Tom Mboya was appointed minister of justice and constitutional affairs in the independence cabinet. In 1964, Mboya became minister of economic planning, a post he held until his assassination on 5 July 1969 at the age of 39.

Mboya was Kenyatta's heir apparent. After he was assassinated, it was said he was the best president Kenya never had.

And together with Oginga Odinga, he will be remembered as a leader who skillfully led the struggle for independence in the 1950s when Jomo Kenyatta was in prison.

Chapter Three:

A Few Years After Independence

SOME of the most important developments in Kenya a few years after independence took place in the political arena.

One was the resignation of Vice President Oginga Odinga who went on to form an opposition party, the Kenya People's Union (KPU), challenging President Kenyatta; and the other one was the easing of tensions in the Northeastern Province following a rapprochement with neighbouring Somalia in 1967, relieving Kenya of a major security and economic problem.

Somalia was the biggest supporter of the Somali rebels in northeastern Kenya who wanted to break away from Kenya and unite with the Somali Republic.

Almost from the beginning, the Kenya People's Union faced formidable challenges because of hostility from the government.

Formed in March 1966, the KPU faced its major test almost exactly three years later when the government in Mach 1968 accused the party of subversion. It was perfect timing, since the KPU was celebrating its third anniversary that month. And it was an anniversary the leaders of the opposition party would never forget.

According to *Africa Contemporary Record: Annual Survey and Documents 1968 – 1969* (p. 156), the government issued an official publication outlining the charges levelled against the Kenya People's Union. The charges were based on what the opposition party members said in parliament since Oginga Odinga formed the party three years earlier.

The charges included "subversive declarations"; "active incitements to revolution or war"; "inflammation of tribal jealousies"; "threats to national security and constitutional government"; and "making a dangerous plaything of politics."

The government document which contained the charges went on to say that it could be assumed that the utterances, which were shielded by parliamentary privilege, "are continually echoed by the KPU members in private discussions or at private meetings around the country."

Like the rest, it was a very serious charge because KPU members were not permitted by the government to address public meetings in their constituencies or or anywhere else including places where public rallies were held.

The document further stated: "The record of KPU members must bring into anxious review the question of the stage at which free speech, as a tool of democracy, may also become a trap into which democracy must fall."

However, the speaker of the Kenyan parliament, Humphrey Slade, warned: "Freedom of speech may, perhaps, be curtailed elsewhere, but freedom of speech in parliament is not only a tool of democracy, it is of the very essence of democracy."

Attorney-General Charles Njonjo said later that the government had no intention of restricting the right members of parliament had to express their views in the national legislature. Yet, only a few days later, his words proved to be no more than empty rhetoric when the deputy leader of the Kenya People's Union, Bildad M. Kaggia, and the chairman of the KPU in South Nyanza, were charged with holding a meeting without permission. It was against the law which the government used effectively to neutralise the opposition.

The two KPU officials were sentenced to 12 months' imprisonment. It was clear that the government was cracking down on the opposition and had no intention of stopping its repressive campaign.

It was also during the same period that Odinga's passport was withdrawn just as he was getting ready to fly to the United States to deliver a lecture at Boston University in the state of Massachusetts. His lecture was entitled, "Revolution As It Affects Newly Independent African States."

Oginga Odinga was also prevented from travelling to Tanzania. He was very close to President Nyerere. It was also Nyerere who wrote the introduction to Odinga's book, *Not Yet Uhuru*, which was not well-received by the Kenyan government. Kenyatta and his colleagues felt that the book's message was a personal attack on them and portrayed the government in a negative way by claiming that Kenyans were not yet free.

Yet, in spite of all this, the opposition was not intimidated into submission. The test of its strength was to have come in June 1968 with local government elections, but the elections were postponed until August because of an amendment to the local government regulations stipulating that only registered political parties would be allowed to nominate candidates for election.

Odinga launched the KPU campaign in August unequivocally stating that the election was a "straight fight" between the KPU and KANU and stressed the unusual importance of that election. It was supposed to be a major test for both parties.

But this was not to be. KPU candidates were "disqualified." The government claimed that they did not comply with the electoral regulations. All KPU candidates were declared to have had their forms filled out "incorrectly." By remarkable contrast, all KANU forms were said to have been completed correctly and in full compliance with election rules.

It was a sign of things to come.

Oginga Odinga described the disqualification of KPU candidates as "illegal and irresponsible" and declared that the KPU would withdraw from all remaining local government nominations and elections. He also said his party would seek legal action.

The secretary-general of KANU, Tom Mboya who coincidentally was a Luo himself like Oginga Odinga, said he personally would have welcomed a full contest throughout the country. He went on to say it was not the intention of the government to ban or destroy the Kenya People's Union; it was the KPU, he claimed, which was not fully prepared for the contest because it lacked the manpower and organisation to cope with a massive exercise of preparing well for such elections.

But there was no question that the government was bent on destroying the Kenya People's Union. And it was not until more than 30 years later that government opponents mobilised forces on a national scale, successfully, and defeated KANU at the polls.

When the KPU was fighting for its life in 1968, there were voices of conscience and moderation in Kenya who wanted the opposition to be given a chance even if some of them were supporters of KANU. According to the independent *Kenya Weekly News*, 21 June 1968:

How will KPU contest the elections if it is not allowed to be organised on a country-wide basis like KANU?....In its brief, but turbulent history, Kenya has had numerous political parties, which in many cases died a natural death. Let KPU follow them into the grave if the *wananchi* do not support its programme after a fair and full hearing of its case. - (*Kenya Weekly News*, quoted in *Africa Contemporary Records: Annual Survey and Documents 1968 – 1969*, p. 157).

About three months later, on 18 September 1968, 20 KPU members of parliament left the opposition party and joined KANU. That was the beginning of the end of the Kenya People's Union.

The 20 KPU members of parliament said they had appealed to Oginga Odinga to dissolve the party and join the government but failed to convince him to do so. Odinga maintained that disbanding the party would be "tantamount to committing political suicide and killing democracy in Kenya."

On 17 September 1968, just one day before 20 KPU members of parliament resigned from the opposition party and joined KANU, the speaker of parliament, Humphrey Slade, announced that the Kenya People's Union could not be recognised as a political party if its membership in parliament dropped below seven. And it did.

The KPU's secretary-general, Christopher Makokna, resigned from the party on 6 December 1968 and rejoined KANU, bringing the number of KPU members of parliament down to six at the end of the year.

The Kenya People's Union was banned in 1969 after political unrest in Nyanza Province, Odinga's home region and a Luo stronghold, during Kenyatta's visit. The two leaders had a bitter verbal exchange in public when Kenyatta was in Nyanza Province during that time, thus inflaming passions on both sides.

That was the end of the Kenya People's Union as a political party in the early years of independence. And no new opposition parties were formed after 1969.

The banning of the KPU was a turning point in the country's history and marked the consolidation of the ruling Kenya African Nation Union (KANU) as the dominant political force in the country, a position it retained for the next 35 years.

It was also important in another fundamental respect: institutionalisation of one-party rule. Although Kenya did not officially become a one-party state until June 1982, it became a de *facto* one-party state after KPU was banned.

Only five years before the Kenya People's Union was banned, another opposition party, the Kenya African Democratic Union (KADU), had also reached it end. That was in 1964.

KADU was the most prominent opposition party before the KPU was formed, and it dissolved itself voluntarily. Its former members joined KANU, not necessarily out of ideological conversion but mainly because of survival. There was no other party they could have joined and which could have posed a credible challenge to KANU.

Led by Ronald Ngala, a former teacher in the Coast Province, KADU was formed to protect the interests of smaller tribes and wanted to have a federal constitution based on provincial governments.

Its members felt that was the best way to protect themselves from domination by the country's large ethnic groups, especially the Kikuyu and the Luo. And they were vindicated by history. For 40 years since independence, the Kikuyu dominated virtually every aspect of Kenyan national life, followed by the Luo.

Chapter Four:

Kenyan Provinces

KENYA is divided into large geographical and administrative units called provinces, roughly equivalent to what Americans call states in their country. In neighbouring Tanzania, they are called regions but were also known as provinces during colonial rule and in the early days of independence.

Kenya has eight provinces. Each province is headed by a provincial commissioner who is appointed by the president, unlike in the United States or in Nigeria where state governors are elected. The city of Nairobi is one of the provinces and we are going to take a look at each one of them.

The Central Province is one of the most well-known provinces in Kenya for a number of reasons. It is the home of the Kikuyu, Kenya's largest ethnic group. It was also the area where Mau Mau was fought in the fifties. The province is also known for its large number of white settlers. Expropriation of land by these settlers, depriving the Kikuyu of their most important asset, triggered the Mau Mau uprising, one of the bloodiest conflicts in colonial history.

Besides the Kikuyu, the Embu and the Meru also claim the Central Province as their ancestral home.

The Central Province covers the area around Nyeri to the southwest of Mount Kenya and is one of the most densely populated areas of Kenya and in the entire East Africa.

Nyeri, which is located north of Nairobi, is the capital of the Central Province. The town lies at the eastern base of the Aberdare mountains, also known as Nyandarua, The mountain range is part of the eastern end of the Great Rift Valley and lies on the western side of Mount Kenya.

Nyeri's tourist attractions include Mount Kenya. And there are many other tourist sites in the area. It is mostly an agricultural district with coffee and tea being the main crops.

The town of Nyeri has a very interesting history. It was established in December 1902 as a garrison during colonial rule but soon became a major trading centre for white farmers in the area. They sold mostly coffee, wheat and cattle. The town also attracted Indian traders.

It was also a major centre of entertainment for whites in those days. They came into town to drink and socialise at the White Rhino Hotel, the Outspan Hotel, and the Aberdare Country Club at nearby Mweiga.

That was life at its best in tropical Africa for the white settlers and many of them still remember those days with nostalgia. The hotels and the country club still exist and are a reminder of "the good old days" decades ago.

Nyeri is also important in the history of Kenya and contemporary national life in another respect. It is the home town of a number of prominent Kenyans. The leader of Mau Mau, Dedan Kimathi, came from Nyeri. Mwai Kibaki, the third president of Kenya after Jomo Kenyatta and Daniel arap Moi, came from Nyeri. And the winner of the Nobel Peace Prize in 2004, Wangari Maathai, also came from Nyeri.

The town of Nyeri has yet another distinction. Just south of the town is Wajee Nature Park. The park is the burial place of Lord Robert Baden-Powell who is known worldwide as the founder of the Boy Scout movement. He also fought in the Boer War in South Africa, one of the bloodiest in the continent's history. He is reported to have written these words about Nyeri: "The nearer to Nyeri, the nearer to bliss."

And he still lies there in eternal bliss.

Baden-Powell's Paxtu cottage, which was converted into a small museum, stands on the grounds of the Outspan Hotel. He and his wife are buried in the town cemetery along with the legendary hunter and conservationist Jim Corbett who is also the author of *Maneaters of Kumaon* which was published in 1944. Corbett also spent his last years in Kenya.

Nyeri has another historical monument of contemporary significance. Only about three miles along the road from where Baden-Powell was buried is the Mathari Mission settlement.

It was built by Italian missionaries in the early 1900s and comprises the Consolata Hospital and School of Nursing. The settlement also has a number of dwellings and other structures. The hospital provides free medical service to the poor in the area and also has facilities for those with money. It is run by nuns of the Consolata order and provides much-needed service without which life for the impoverished would be much harder.

The town of Nyeri and its surrounding areas is a condensed version of the Central Province. It is a fertile province. So is Nyeri. The province is also a major tourist attraction. And so is Nyeri.

Sitting in the foothills of the Aberdares, it is surrounded by extensive green meadows and gardens.

The foothills are also covered by a dense eucalyptus forest and provides a magnificent view of Mount Kenya, the highest in the country and one of the tallest on the entire continent.

Besides the extensive farmland surrounding the town and which is known for its coffee and tea, Nyeri also is known as a vibrant commercial centre whose major industries include the production of leather goods, soap, wood and furniture, processed food, soft drinks, cord, rope, twine, clay and concrete products, agricultural implements, and fabrics.

Nyeri also is the gateway to Aberdare National Park. The town is linked by road and railway with Nanyuki, another important town which is about 36 miles to the northeast, and with Nairobi about 60 miles to the southwest.

Nyeri's climate also reminds one of the weather conditions throughout the province. Because of its higher altitude, the climate of the Central Province is generally cooler than that of the rest of Kenya and is the main reason why a disproportionately large number of whites decided to settle in the region.

There is of plenty of rain in the Central Province, from March to May, and again from October to November, making it one of the most fertile areas on the entire continent.

The Central Province is not only the biggest producer of coffee and tea in Kenya; it is also the headquarters of the dairy industry in the country. No other province produces more dairy products, and no other province is more endowed in terms of agricultural potential as the producer of Kenya's most important export crops and some of the biggest foreign exchange earners.

The Central Province is divided into seven districts: Nyandarua whose capital is Ol Kalou; Nyeri, with Nyeri as its capital; Kirinyaga, with the capital being Kerugoya; Maragua – capital Maragua; Murang'a, with Murang'a as its capital; Thika, whose capital is also called Thika and after which the district is named as is the case with most of them across the country; and Kiambu, with Kiambu as its capital. Kiambu also is the home district of the founding father of the nation, Mzee Jomo Kenyatta, and many other prominent national leaders.

And the province will always remain an important part of the history of Kenya and the struggle for independence. Had a lot of fertile land in the Central Province not been taken away from the Kikuyu - and to a smaller degree from the Embu and the Meru as well - by the British settlers; and had the province not been dominated by whites, there probably would have been no Mau Mau and the history of Kenya would have been different.

Much of the province was designated "White Highlands" to be used exclusively by white settlers. Other parts of Kenya in the Rift Valley Province were also exclusively reserved for whites as an integral part of what whites considered to be the white man's land.

But it was the Central Province which was the epicentre of seismic activity that rocked the entire nation during the Mau Mau uprising triggered by racial injustice against Africans.

Expropriation of land was at the core of this conflict. It embodied all the injustices Africans suffered and was the highest expression of European arrogance. Kenya was an African country. Yet European settlers said it was the white man's land. Africans wanted equality and justice. Europeans were determined to dominate them and perpetuate white minority rule.

When the British East Africa colony (later renamed Kenya) was founded in 1905, the colonial government encouraged the British to immigrate to the colony in order to establish a white nation in the tropics.

By 1920, when the territory became the Kenya Colony, about 10,000 British settlers had established themselves in the country. And there was nothing to stop them from acquiring land on their own terms, disregarding the interests of Africans. They got 999-year leases over 25 percent of some of the most fertile land in Kenya.

The result was Mau Mau in which the tribes which were affected the most – the Kikuyu, the Embu, and Meru – were actively involved.

They were forcibly removed from their ancestral homes and relocated in natives reserves which were nothing but concentration camps reminiscent of Nazi Germany. As the country approached independence, there were about 60,000 whites in Kenya.

The land they owned had also been taken away from other indigenous people. Among the other victims were the Kamba, and the Maasai - probably the most well-known African pastoralists who found the amount of grazing land drastically reduced as the area designated as the "White Highlands" expanded to affect them as well.

The temperate climate of the highlands made them not only suitable but even more attractive to whites. They were also very fertile, with volcanic soil, and with all the potential for a highly prosperous future.

A large number of the white settlers came from South Africa, and their presence and impact through the years since they first arrived is still felt today in the Rift Valley Province with the town of Eldoret, founded by the Boers, being the most visible symbol of their impact and influence.

Forced labour, extracted from Africans through taxation and by other means, only made things worse in terms of race relations, adding fuel to the fire.

It was not until the mid- and late fifties that whites began to make some concessions to Africans as the nationalist tide sweeping across the country - and the rest of the continent - forced them to eventually relinquish control. As *Time* magazine stated in a report entitled, "Opening the White Highlands," in its edition of 20 June 1955 when Mau Mau was going on:

In colonial Kenya, the best farmlands are the Highlands, known as the White Highlands because only white settlers are permitted to own land there.

Forty-three thousand whites share about 12,000 sq. mi. of the Highlands, while the colony's 5,300,000 Africans are crowded into 52,000 sq. mi. of less desirable farmlands down below, or scrabble for their living in the arid, underdeveloped 'Crown Lands' —a euphemism for wilderness.

For many years the million-strong Kikuyu tribe, less uneducated than most and peacefully inclined, talked hopefully of expanding their holdings into the White Highlands; instead, the white settlers told them to go expand into the Crown Lands, and vaguely talked of irrigation projects that would some day make the Crown Lands bloom.

Frustrated, many of the Kikuyu farmers turned to other occupations, including joining the Mau Mau and beheading whites.

Two years ago, Britain's Tory government, while busy fighting off the Mau Mau, appointed a Royal Commission to take a long, slow look at the East African problem. Last week, in a thoroughgoing, 482-page report, the Royal Commission made one overriding recommendation: the White Highlands must be opened up to African ownership, and African land ghettoes must be done away with.

As for the Africans, the commission urged them to drop their old ways of tribal land ownership, and to switch to individual or family land ownership.

Considering that the Mau Mau shooting war is still on, and that Kenya's black v. white feeling runs high, the Royal Commission's report had a Utopian and distant sound about it.

The diehard majority of British settlers is sure to oppose it, and to try to sabotage any attempt at implementation; the settlers can say, with reason, that conditions for peaceful transfer of land between races do not now exist.

But some day soon in darkest East Africa, a start must somehow be made; something new must be offered the Africans in place of blood-cults and drums, prejudice and pangas flashing in the night.

In a subsequent report – a few years later – with the same title, "Opening the White Highlands," *Time* had this to say in its 26 October 1959 edition:

'Hello—have you sold your farm yet?'
In Kenya last week, this was the standard greeting whenever white settlers met. Behind it lay the bitterest blow that Kenya's settlers have yet suffered: a Kenya government proposal to open up to Africans and Asians the immensely fertile 12,700 sq. mi. of the British colony's 'White Highlands.'

The White Highlands are "white" because since 1939 only Kenya's 60,000 Europeans have been allowed to lease farms there—a state of affairs that has constituted a perennial political and psychological affront to the colony's 6,000,000 Africans.

The new plan might ease the affront, but even its proponents did not argue that it would admit more than a sprinkling of non-Europeans into the Highlands. As the plan now stands, an African farmer who wanted to move into the Highlands would first have to get financing, then find a European farmer who was willing to sell his lease to a nonwhite, and finally, make a convincing demonstration of his agricultural know-how to an 'area control board' dominated by European settlers.

The one limitation on the area control boards: any African or Asian who suspected that his application had been refused on racial grounds could appeal to a central control board made up of Asians, Africans and Europeans in equal number.

Mild as it was, the new plan pleased no one. Said Group Captain Leslie Briggs, hard-shell leader of the far-right, pure-white United Party: 'This is dishonest and dangerous—we would have no right to stop a convicted Mau Mau gangster farming next door to us.'

With equal vehemence, African Nationalist Leader Tom Mboya denounced the proposals as falling far short of the sweeping redistribution of White Highlands acreage demanded by Africans.

Even members of the moderate New Kenya Party, led by Michael Blundell, Kenya's most progressive white politician, raised the outcry that the plan was discriminatory against Europeans; it was unfair, they said, to open the Highlands to Africans, when white farmers were not allowed to buy any of the thousands of fertile acres lying unused in African tribal reserves.

At week's end, in a naked bid for the support of the New Kenya Party, the government announced that henceforth African land boards would no longer be allowed to bar land sales to white farmers on racial grounds. And if it chose, the government could almost certainly push its new plan for the Highlands through Kenya's Legislative Council.

But in the process, it might well increase rather than diminish the tension between Kenya's races. Departing Kenya Governor Sir Evelyn Baring, mused the London *Times*, had handed to his successor, Sir Patrick Renison, 'a baton . . . that looks suspiciously like a stick of dynamite.'

The Central Province played a key role in this political awakening and nationalist agitation among Africans, helping to mobilise forces transcending ethnic and regional differences across the country.

And while the Central Province can indeed be described as just another Kenyan province, it is equally true that the unique role it played in the history of the country distinguishes it from the other provinces.

And it will always stand out as a monument not only to the struggle for independence in Kenya but throughout the continent, earning Mzee Jomo Kenyatta distinction as the Grand Old Man of the African independence movement and one of the most revered statesmen Africa has ever produced.

It was also in the Central Province where the nation's capital, Nairobi, was built. And it enjoyed that distinction, as the home of the nation's capital, until Nairobi itself was elevated to the status of province.

We are now going to look at the Coast Province whose coastal area played the most important role in the penetration of the interior.

It was the entry point, and almost all foreigners who came to what later became Kenya embarked on their journeys into the interior from the coast, especially from Mombasa. Therefore the Coast Province will always occupy a unique place in the history of Kenya, not only in terms of penetration but colonisation by Europeans.

Mombasa is the capital of the Coast Province. It is Kenya's second largest city and has one of the largest ports on the entire continent. It also has an international airport and is a bustling centre of the tourism industry, one of the most vibrant in East Africa.

The city of Mombasa is located on an island, which is also called Mombasa, and is separated from the mainland by two creeks: Tudor Creek and Kilindini Harbour. But the city also extends to the mainland although it is centred on Mombasa island.

Kilindini Harbour is a large, natural deep-water inlet extending inland from Mombasa. The harbour is the main part of the port of Mombasa.

Mombasa has a long history, going back for centuries, as a city and as a harbour. Kilindini Harbour was inaugurated in 1896 when work started on the construction of the Kenya-Uganda Railway which went on play a major role in the history of Kenya and Uganda by opening up the interior and paving the way for the colonisation of the two countries.

Today it continues to play an important role as the life line for both countries and their only outlet to the sea. Without the railway, neither country would have a major access to the sea.

Mombasa also played a very important role during World War II when Kilindini served as a temporary base for the British Eastern Fleet from the beginning of 1942 until the Japanese naval threat to Colombo, Ceylon (now Sri Lanka), had been neutralised. It was also at Kilindini where the British had a code-breaking operation during the war when they succeeded in breaking Japanese naval codes.

So, Mombasa not only played a major role in the colonisation of Kenya but also helped save the British Empire during World War II.

Mombasa is a predominantly Muslim city inhabited by the Swahili, a coastal people who are a product of Arab culture and in many cases of intermarriage between Arabs and Africans.

Through the centuries, the marriage was one-sided in the sense that it was Arab men who married African women or had them as concubines. It was extremely rare for black men to marry Arab women although there were illicit relations between them through the years.

That was mainly because of racism. Arab men felt that black men were not good enough to marry Arab women, and Arab women felt the same way about black men. And it is a stereotype that persists unto this day, although there has been more racial intermingling and even interracial marriage through the years – much more than before.

Mombasa has for centuries been a kind of melting pot in tropical Africa. It has attracted immigrants from the Middle East and India through the centuries, making the city a kind of laboratory for experiments in human relations across racial lines. The racial intermingling has contributed to a rich cultural diversity virtually unmatched anywhere else along the East African coast with the possible exception of Dar es Salaam in neighbouring Tanzania.

In recent years, a large number of immigrants have come from the hinterland, bringing with them their traditions and cultures which have added to the cultural diversity and vitality of Mombasa.

But it also has been an explosive mix, at times, as tragically demonstrated by the ethnic clashes in the late 1990s which were fuelled by unscrupulous politicians who exploited the xenophobic fear among many coastal residents who felt that they were being invaded and overwhelmed by "foreigners" from other parts of Kenya, especially the interior.

The people along the coast, including Mombasa, are known for their traditional attire which has been heavily influenced by Islamic culture since the vast majority of the people themselves are Muslim.

A very large number of men wear a long dress known as *kanzu* in Kiswahili, usually accompanied by a Muslim cap. Muslim women wear a loose cloth known as *bui bui*, which is traditionally black, along with a head covering. The women also wrap themselves in a cotton cloth called *kanga* in Kiswahili. The cloth usually has highly inspirational words printed on it. They are mostly Swahili sayings, including proverbs, full of wisdom.

The Muslims along the coast in Tanzania have the same attire.

Mombasa has many interesting places to visit. They include Fort Jesus, built by the Portuguese, and the Old Town which is full of Islamic architecture built centuries ago.

Fort Jesus was built in 1593 as a fortress against invaders in order to protect the old port of Mombasa.

Between 1631 and 1875, it became a focal point in conflicts between many competing forces who wanted to take over Mombasa. It was declared a historical monument in 1958 and is a museum today. But it will always be remembered as one of the finest examples of sixteenth-century Portuguese military architecture.

Cannons and cannon balls from a bygone era are some of the reminders of the important role Fort Jesus played in the history of Mombasa. They are some of the major attractions at the fort and remind visitors of the long history of this important city on the East African coast. Fort Jesus attracts hundreds of thousands of visitors, including scholars, from all over the world every year and is one of the most well-known tourist destinations in East Africa.

There would, of course, have been no Fort Jesus without Mombasa whose founding is associated with two rulers: Mwana Mkisi, a female, and Shehe Mvita.

Old Mombasa had trade links not only with the Middle East and India but also with China. The Portuguese explorer Vasco da Gama was the first known European to visit Mombasa in 1498. Mombasa was also the first capital of the British East Africa Protectorate which later came to be known as Kenya.

As a coastal city, Mombasa has a hot and sometimes humid climate. It also gets a significant amount of rain especially in April and May.

As a cultural attraction, Mombasa stands out in one respect among all the towns and cities in Kenya. It is the centre of Taarab music which originated from Zanzibar and is basically Arab.

Other important towns in the Coast Province along the coast include Diani in the south, and Malindi, Watamu and Lamu in the north.

Diani has developed into a major tourist centre, with palm trees and white sandy beaches like Mombasa.

Founded by the Arabs, Malindi is an old historic town

which has been a Swahili settlement since the 14th century. Once rivalled only by Mombasa for dominance in this part of East Africa, the town attracted foreign powers through the centuries because of its strategic location and its significance as a port.

In 1414, Chinese explorer Zheng He visited Malindi with his fleet and the ruler of Malindi sent a personal envoy together with a giraffe as a present to China on that fleet when it returned home.

It was also in Malindi where Vasco da Gama picked up his sea pilot who used the monsoon winds to help the Portuguese explorer get to India. When he first arrived in Malindi in 1498, he signed a trade agreement with the rulers of the town and hired a guide for his voyage to India. And in the following year, the Portuguese established a trading post in Malindi which served as a refueling stop - for food, water and other basic necessities - on the way to and from India.

Many old buildings still exist in Malindi today and are one of the town's major attractions. They include a mosque and a palace on the beach. Not only is Malindi a major historic site and tourist attraction; it is also one of the most well-known towns in the entire East Africa. Its history has been a confluence of major cultural tributaries: African, Arab, Chinese, Indian, and European, among others.

Other places of interest and major tourist attractions in Malindi include beaches fringed with palm trees; Watamu and Malindi Marine Parks, the first of their kind in Africa; and the Gede Ruins in Gede which dates back to the 13th century.

Gede was abandoned in the early 1600s, although no one knows exactly why. It is assumed that the town was invaded and plundered by unknown invaders. Another school of thought contends that the inhabitants abandoned the town after their wells lost water when the ocean receded.

Whatever the case, the abandoned settlement became

ruins and a major tourist attraction. In 1927, the Gede ruins were declared a historic monument. They include pillar tombs, a mosque and the palace. There is also a Nature Trail around the inner and outer walls. And the museum has many artifacts including Chinese and Phoenician porcelain excavated from the ruins.

Without Malindi, the history of Kenya is incomplete. And without Malindi, one can not get a comprehensive picture of the life and cultural diversity in the Coast Province, one of the most dynamic regions on the entire East African coast.

Another important town on the northern coastal strip of Kenya is Watamu. It is a small fishing community but of singular significance as East Africa's first Marine National Park.

Then there is the town of Lamu. It is the largest town on Lamu Island and is on the *World Heritage List*. It is also the capital of Lamu District.

Lamu District is part of the Lamu Archipelago. The district covers a strip of the northeastern coastal area of the mainland and Lamu Islands.

The islands are close to the border with Somalia. The largest of the islands are Pate, Manda, and Lamu.

The archipelago contains many important historical and archaelogical sites which include Takwa and Manda Town, both on Manda Island, and Shanga on Pate Island. Excavation of the sites through the years has provided profound insights into Swahili history and culture which goes back for centuries long before the advent of colonial rule.

Takwa, which is in ruins today, was founded around 1500. It was never a large place and was abandoned around 1700. One of the most important remains in Takwa is the Great Mosque which is relatively well-preserved. Another important structure is the Pillar Tomb. It has an inscription with the date of 1681 – 1682.

Historians and archaelogists have speculated   that

Takwa was a place of worship or where religious leaders went to pray. It has also been reported that when Takwa was abandoned, its inhabitants settled just across the bay at Shela on Lamu Island.

Even today, the people of Shela go to the Pillar Tomb twice a year to pray for rain.

Shela is a village about two miles from the town of Lamu. The village is also a centre for tourism on the island. It is also home to the most spectacular beaches on Lamu Island. Traditional dhows are a sight to behold and remind one of a bygone era before Western civilisation was brought to East Africa.

Manda Town, one of the great historic sites on the entire East African coast, also lies in ruins today. The town owes its origin to commercial activities between the coastal people and traders from the Persian Gulf in the 9th and 10th centuries and was a thriving community in its heyday.

Items found during excavations in Manda Town include Chinese porcelain dating from the 9th century onwards, Islamic pottery and glass and local pottery. The town also has large sea walls.

It has another distinctive feature. Almost right from the beginning when the town was founded, the inhabitants of Manda used burnt bricks and stone to build their houses. They also used lime to hold stones together.

The employment of these techniques and skills has been found only on the coast and on the islands of Kenya in the nation's early history. Nothing of the sort was used in other parts of what is Kenya today during that period long before colonial rule.

Manda Town prospered until the 13th century. It had reached its peak and began to go downhill. It was finally abandoned in the first half of the 19th century due to lack of water.

Another very important historical and archaelogical site in the Lamu Archipelago is Shanga on Pate Island.

Excavation at the site shows that the earliest settlement took place in the 8th century and a small number of local inhabitants were Muslim. Locally minted coins and burial sites have also been found at Shanga. Members of an Arab tribe arrived at Shanga and other parts of the coast and introduced a new form of government.

Shanga was finally abandoned between 1400 and 1425 and some descendants of the original inhabitants still live in the nearby town of Siyu and are known as Washanga in Kiswahili, which means the people Shanga.

But besides Mombasa, and Zanzibar in Tanzania, no other town on the East African coast stands out as Lamu does.

It was founded in the 14th century and contains many buildings typical of Swahili architecture. The old city is described in the *World Heritage List* as "the oldest and best-preserved Swahili settlement in East Africa." And it is, of course, the largest town on Lamu Island.

It was once a thriving centre for the slave trade conducted by the Arabs and has an interesting ethnic mix partly because of this traffic in human beings, and partly because of the trade links it had with Asia and with the Middle East for centuries.

And because it interacted heavily with the Arab nations in the Persian Gulf, it was greatly influenced by Islam which led to the development of a predominantly Muslim community not only in the town of Lamu but on the entire island and in most parts of the coastal region.

Ironically, the first area to be penetrated by Europeans including missionaries who were also the first to build schools, ended up being the least developed in terms of education.

That was mainly because the people in the coastal regions throughout East Africa were mostly Muslim, while the harbingers of Western civilisation were Christian and admitted into their schools Christian converts almost to the total exclusion of everybody else including Muslims.

And even today, Lamu and many other coastal areas are some of the least cosmopolitan parts of the country in terms of Western civilisation.

The town of Lamu is in many fundamental respects a relic from the past, yet at the same time it stands out as one of the best examples of communities which have been able to resist outside influence, retaining their true identities. The resiliency of its culture through the centuries has been remarkable.

Cars are not allowed, partly because of the town's narrow streets but probably mainly because the people of Lamu don't want to lose their identity and way of life they have enjoyed for centuries. This is one of the best cases in which people have demonstrated that simplicity is a virtue, and that tampering with their past is tantamount to giving up their true identity.

Lack of transport is not a problem. The town of Lamu is easily explored by foot. Or you can use a bicycle. Many local residents prefer riding donkeys.

Besides Lamu, Malindi and Mombasa, the other districts which also collectively constitute the Coast Province are Kilifi whose capital is Kilifi; Kwale, with Kwale town being the administrative headquarters; Taita-Taveta, with Wundanyi as its capital; and Tana River whose district headquarters is Hola.

Next, our survey of Kenya takes us to the Eastern Province.

It is the second-largest province in terms of area. Embu is the provincial capital. It is a large town about 75 miles northeast of Nairobi as you go towards Mount Kenya. The mountain is located about 95 miles northeast of Nairobi in central Kenya.

Embu is also the main trading centre in eastern Kenya and also for the Embu tribe of central Kenya. It was founded in 1906 by the British settlers.

It is also one of the most fascinating towns in terms of scenic beauty. It is known for its jacaranda trees which literally turn the town into a purple shower when they flower. It is stunning beauty. The jacaranda trees lose their green leaves and become solid purple when they bloom, usually in October-November each year, depending on rainfall.

Embu also has one of the biggest churches in Africa, the Anglican's Saint Paul's Cathedral with a unique African-inspired design.

The Embu people, after whom the town is named, are concentrated in Embu District which is also one of the districts in the Eastern Province. The town of Embu is also the district headquarters as much as it is the provincial capital.

The Embu are surrounded by a number of tribes. They include their cousins, the Mbeere in Mbeere District to the south. The Embu and the Mbeere once lived in the same district, Embu District, and were collectively known as the Embu until the district was split into two for administrative convenience due to increased population and other factors.

To the west of the Embu are the Kikuyu in Kirinyaga and Nyeri districts. And to the east are the Meru in Meru South District.

Some of the most distinctive features of the Eastern Province include its boundary with Ethiopia to the north; Mount Kenya, the Chalbi Desert, and the eastern half of Lake Turkana. The climate is arid and semi-arid.

Mount Kenya is the highest mountain in Kenya and the second-highest in Africa after Mount Kilimanjaro in neighbouring Tanzania. And it is one of the biggest tourist attractions in the country. It is an extinct volcano and has glaciers. The mountain has also been designated as a world heritage site by UNESCO.

The main ethnic groups living around Mount Kenya are the Kikuyu, the Embu, the Kamba, and the Maasai, and they all see it as an integral part of their lives and cultures.

The Kikuyu live on the southern and eastern sides of

the mountain and they are mostly farmers. The volcanic ash on the lower slopes of the mountain provide them with fertile soil for their crops.

According to traditional Kikuyu beliefs, the creator of the Kikuyu, known as *Ngai* in their language, lives on Mount Kenya; a sentiment also forcefully articulated by Jomo Kenyatta in his classic work and best-selling book *Facing Mount Kenya*

The Kikuyu build their houses with the doors facing Mount Kenya, and their name for this mountain is Kirinyaga, which means the "white" or "bright" mountain, probably because of its snow, although the term may have a deeper meaning for them in religious terms, but not that God is white.

The Embu, who are closely related to the Kikuyu, also believe that their creator, *Ngai* (which is the same name their cousins the Kikuyu use), lives on Mount Kenya. Therefore the mountain is equally sacred to them and they also build their houses with the doors facing the mountain just like the Kikuyu do. The Embu name for Mount Kenya is Kirenia, which means mountain of whiteness.

To the Maasai, who originally came from Sudan like the Luo did, the mountain also has religious significance and a highly symbolic meaning in their lives. They believe that their ancestors came down from the mountain at the beginning of time, although this belief is not supported by historical evidence of the origin of the Maasai further north in Sudan.

The Maasai have two names for Mount Kenya. They call it Ol Donyo Eibor, which means white mountain; they also call it Ol Donyo Egere, meaning speckled mountain. Both mean basically the same thing.

The Kamba also have two names for Mount Kenya. They call it Kima Ja Kengria, which means mountain of whiteness. They also call it Kiinyaa, meaning the mountain of the ostrich. The reference to the ostrich has to do with the colour of the mountain peaks. They are white with snow and dark with rock, making them look similar to the tail feathers of the male ostrich.

The Kamba, also known as Wakamba, are the biggest ethnic group in the Eastern Province. We are going to take a look at them in more detail later when we look at other groups or tribes across the country.

Besides Mount Kenya, the other highly prominent physical feature of the Eastern Province is Lake Turkana, half of which lies in the province.

Lake Turkana is in the Great Rift Valley which includes the Eastern Province. The northern end of the lake crosses into Ethiopia. Therefore the lake is shared by the two East African countries.

Lake Turkana enjoys the distinction of being the world's largest permanent desert lake and the world's largest alkaline lake. The people in the area use the water for various activities but it's not suitable for drinking because of its high alkaline content.

The lake supports a wide range of lacustrine life, and it is in an area where the climate is hot and very dry.

The rocks in the area of the lake are mainly volcanic and there is one active volcano, Central Island, which emits vapours.

People visiting the area have to be fully aware of the weather conditions because on-shore and off-shore winds can be extremely strong. That's because the lake warms and cools more slowly than the land. Sudden, violent storms are frequent and can be dangerous if the people visiting the area are not cautious.

Three rivers flow into Lake Turkana. They are Omo, Turkwel, and Kerio. But no water flows out of the lake. Therefore evaporation is the only way the lake looses water.

The Omo River is not in Kenya; it's in Ethiopia and therefore flows into the lake from the Ethiopian side of the border. It is in the southern part of Ethiopia and is a perennial river.

The Turkwel River flows from Mount Elgon in western Kenya and empties into Lake Turkana in the east. Mount Elgon is on the Kenyan-Ugandan border. The name Turkwel means "river of many fish" in the Turkana language, which is the language of one of Kenya's 42 (or about 50) ethnic groups or tribes.

The Kerio River, which also flows into Lake Turkana, originates from the Rift Valley Province and is one of the longest in Kenya.

Lake Turkana has another attractive feature: Nile crocodiles which are found in abundance in the lake. It once contained the largest population of Nile crocodiles.

The lake and the surrounding areas are a popular destination for tourists. But the expeditions can be dangerous without the help of guides, rangers and experienced persons.

There are also parks in the area: Lake Turkana National Park which is listed by UNESCO as a world heritage site; Sibiloi National Park on the eastern shore of the lake; and Central Island National Park as well as South Island National Park both of which lie in the lake and are known for their crocodiles.

The former name of the lake has an interesting history. It was named Lake Rudolph in honour of Crown Prince Rudolf of Austria in 1888 and retained the name until it was renamed Lake Turkana in 1975, twelve years after independence. The Turkana call the lake, *anam Ka'alakol*, which means "the sea of many fish."

The two European explorers - one Austrian and one Hungarian - who named it Lake Rudolph claimed they discovered it in March 1888, although the indigenous people knew about the lake all the time and were the first to see it.

But that is how the history of exploration of Africa by Europeans was written - by Europeans - until Africans themselves began to write their own history and correct some of these historical "facts."

In fact, the history written about Africa by Europeans when they first went to Africa and even during colonial rule as well as after independence is not African history but the history of Europeans in Africa. And it is written from their perspective to suit their own interpretation of historical facts about Africans and the continent.

But that is another subject. A whole book can be written about it.

Anyway, back to Kenya and our discussion of the Turkana region.

The indigenous people who live in the area of Lake Turkana and other parts and who have always known about the lake include the Turkana, after whom the lake is named; the Rendille, the Gabbra, the Daasanach, the Hamar Koke, the Karo, the Nyagatom, the Mursi, the Surma, and the Molo.

The lake is also famous for its birds. Hundreds of species are found in the area. The East African Rift System also serves as a flyway for migrating birds, bringing in hundreds more.

Animals found in large numbers in the area around the lake include zebras, gazelles, giraffes, lions and cheetahs, and the topi.

There are other major lakes in Kenya besides Lake Turkana. They include Lake Naivasha, Lake Nakuru, Lake Baringo, Lake Bogoria, and Lake Logipi. They are all Rift Valley lakes in what is specifically known as the Eastern Rift Valley which also extends to Tanzania.

Altogether, there are eight lakes in the Kenyan section of the Eastern Rift Valley. Two are freshwater and the rest alkaline.

Lake Turkana is the largest of the Kenyan lakes. It is alkaline. Lake Baringo is the second largest of the Kenyan Rift Valley lakes and is freshwater. The only other freshwater lake in the Kenyan Eastern Rift Valley is Lake Naivasha.

The other alkaline lakes besides Lake Turkana are Lake

Logipi, a seasonal, shallow hot-spring fed soda lake in the Suguta Valley just south of Lake Turkana; Lake Bogoria, a shallow soda lake which is also a national preserve; Lake Nakuru, a shallow soda lake whose area around it together with the lake itself has also been a national park since 1968; Lake Elmenteita, a shallow soda lake; and Lake Magadi, which is also a shallow soda lake. In fact, the word *magadi* means soda ash in Kiswahili.

But it is Lake Turkana which stands out among all these lakes because of its size, and also because it is shared by two countries, Kenya and Ethiopia. It is also a great asset to the Eastern Province which we have just looked at in our survey of Kenyan provinces.

The Eastern Province has 13 districts. They are – together with their capitals: Embu – capital Embu; Isiolo – capital Isiolo; Kitui – capital Kitui; Machakos – capital Machakos; Makueni – capital Wote; Marsabit – capital Marsabit; Mbeere – capital Siakago; Meru Central – capital Meru; Meru North, also known as Nyambene District, with Maua as its capital; Meru South, also known as Nithi District, with Chuka as the capital; Moyale – capital Moyale; Mwingi – capital Mwingi; and Tharaka whose capital is also named Tharaka.

The Eastern Province also enjoys the distinction of being home to the first capital of Kenya: Machakos.

The town of Machakos, which is surrounded by hilly terrain and whose indigenous people are the Akamba(s) also known as the Kamba or Wakamba, was established in 1889, ten years before Nairobi was built.

It was the first administrative centre for British East Africa, later renamed Kenya, but the colonial rulers moved the capital to Nairobi in 1899 because Machakos by-passed the Uganda Railway that was under construction during that time.

Otherwise it probably would have remained Kenya's capital and very likely would have been the country's capital even today had it not been bypassed by the railway from Mombasa to Kisumu.

The town and the district were named after Masaku, a Kamba chief, and the name Machakos is a corruption - by the British - of the original name.

There is also a place in one of the hills around the town of Machakos which is famous for "water flowing against gravity." It is located on Kituluni Hill, 12 miles east of Machakos town.

Next we go to Nairobi Province which is also home to Kenya's capital Nairobi.

Nairobi Province shares boundaries with the city of Nairobi but functions as a regional administrative unit separate from the city of Nairobi, although it is named after the capital. And it is headed by a provincial commissioner just like any other Kenyan province.

But Nairobi Province differs from the other provinces in several ways. It is the smallest province in terms of area; it is entirely urban because of Kenya's capital Nairobi; and it has only one local authority, Nairobi City, and only one district, Nairobi District. But like all the other districts in Kenya, it is further divided into "divisions" which are further divided into "locations."

The city of Nairobi is a bustling metropolis and the most cosmopolitan of all the cities in East Africa. In fact, it is one of the most cosmopolitan on the entire continent like many cities in South Africa, and Abidjan in the Ivory Coast.

Founded in 1899, it is popularly known as the "Green City in the Sun," a name derived from the city's foliage and warm climate, and is the most populous city in East Africa.

It became the capital of Kenya in 1905 after Mombasa lost that status when the colonial authorities decided to transfer the capital from the coast to the interior and chose Nairobi to be the new administrative centre for the new colony.

The city of Nairobi is also the capital of Nairobi

Province, and Nairobi District.

The city lies on Nairobi River and enjoys a cool climate because of its high altitude.

It is one of the most prominent cities on the continent and in the entire Third World and has offices of many international companies and organisations including the United Nations.

In terms of commercial activities, it is the capital of East Africa although the East African Community (EAC) has its headquarters in Arusha in northern Tanzania.

The origin of Nairobi is inextricably linked with the history of colonisation in Kenya. The area of what came to be Nairobi was basically a swampy area, and uninhabited, until 1899 when a supply depot for the Uganda Railway – also known as the Kenya/Uganda Railway – was built. The depot soon became the railway headquarters.

The city was named after a water hole known in Maasai as *Ewaso Nyirobi* which means "cool water." It was hit by a catastrophe in its early years and was totally rebuilt in the early 1900s after an outbreak of plague and the burning of the original town.

The area of Nairobi was chosen as the supply depot for the railway during its construction, and as the railway headquarters, because of its central location between Mombasa and Kampala (Uganda).

It was also chosen because its network of rivers could supply the camp with water, and its elevation would make it cool enough for Europeans who preferred a cooler climate at higher altitudes somewhat reminiscent of the temperate climate in Europe.

The location was also chosen for health reasons. The tropics are notorious for malaria but at such a high altitude, mosquitoes would not be able to survive in large numbers and be a danger to the residents of the area.

Nairobi River, which flows through the city, is the main river of the Nairobi river basin which is a complex of several streams flowing eastwards. All of the Nairobi basin rivers join east of Nairobi and meet the Athi River, eventually flowing to the Indian Ocean. The water from this river proved to be critical to the survival of Nairobi especially during the founding of the settlement and the early years.

When Nairobi became the capital of the British protectorate (British East Africa) in 1905, it started to grow mainly because it was the administrative centre and a tourist destination. The tourism industry was initially in the form of big game hunting and attracted many hunters including some of the most famous.

The town grew further when the colonial rulers started to explore the region, using Nairobi as their launching pad and operational centre. This prompted the colonial government to build several major hotels in the town. The main occupants of these hotels were British game hunters, joined by Americans and others in subsequent years.

The town continued to grow during colonial rule and British settlers settled in Nairobi and the surrounding areas. A large number of Britons were already being encouraged to immigrate to Kenya and acquire land and Nairobi was the first town in the interior they went to. But the expansion of the town put them on a collision course with the Kikuyu and the Maasai whose land was being expropriated by the colonial government to satisfy colonial ambitions.

And it witnessed rapid growth. In 1919, it was declared a municipality. Between 1920 and 1950, the number of white settlers within Nairobi rose from 9,000 to 80,000. But friction between the settlers and the indigenous people who had lost their land continued through the years as whites demanded and expropriated more and more land, while the town also continued to expand. It became a city in 1954.

Nairobi's location – it is adjacent to the Rift Valley – makes it prone to earthquakes. But only minor quakes and tremors occur occasionally.

The famous Ngong Hills – mentioned in a number of books by colonial settlers – which are located to the west of the city are the most prominent geographical feature of the Nairobi area.

During colonial rule, the area around Ngong Hills was a major settler farming region and many traditional colonial houses are still seen in the area. In the 1985 film *Out of Africa*, the four peaks of the Ngong Hills appear in the background of several scenes near Karen Blixen's house. Local residents still reported seeing lions in the Hills during the 1990s.

Ngong is a Maasai word which means "knuckles." Near the hills is the town of Ngong, not far from Nairobi whose background of Ngong Hills is very much an integral part of this metropolis.

Also, both Mount Kenya north of Nairobi and Mount Kilimanjaro to the southeast in Tanzania are visible from Nairobi on a clear day.

Nairobi has many parks and open spaces and the city has dense tree-cover.

The most famous park is Uhuru Park adjacent to the central business district. It is the largest park and has an artificial lake and an assembly ground for political rallies and religious gatherings.

Then there is Central Park close to Uhuru Park. It includes a memorial for Jomo Kenyatta. Other well-known open spaces in Nairobi include City Park, Nairobi Arboretum, and Jeevanjee Gardens.

As a major metropolis with a cosmopolitan outlook, Nairobi is also a multicultural city. And it has maintained a strong British presence since its founding more than 100 years ago.

Many foreigners from other British colonies settled in Nairobi through the years, adding to the racial and cultural diversity of the town. The majority of these immigrants came from India and Pakistan to build the Kenya-Uganda

Railway from Mombasa to Kisumu and they ended up settling in Nairobi after the railway was completed.

The city also has long-established communities from Somalia and Sudan.

There are also a number of churches, mosques and temples and other houses of worship and cultural centres reflecting the multicultural composition of this vibrant city. Prominent places of worship in the city include the Holy Family Basilica Cathedral, All Saints Cathedral, Jamia Mosque, and Ismaili Jamat Khana.

Nairobi's image as a cultural centre is also reflected in films, one of the most famous being *Out of Africa* which is also the name of the book on which the film is based.

The book was written by Karen Blixen, whose pen name was Isak Dinesen, and it is an account of her life in Kenya and her impressions of this land of majestic beauty in the tropics. She lived in the Nairobi area from 1917 to 1931 and the neighbourhood in which she lived, Karen, is named after her. The popularity of the film prompted the opening of the Karen Blixen Museum in Nairobi.

The city is also the setting of many works by Ngugi wa Thiong'o, Kenya's most prominent author and one of Africa's most distinguished writers comparable to Chinua Achebe and Wole Soyinka as a literary giant.

Nairobi is also an important tourist destination. The most prominent tourist attraction is the Nairobi National Park. The park is unique in the sense that it is the only game reserve of this nature to border a nation's capital city or a city of this size. At this writing, Nairobi had a population of about 4 million people.

The park has many animals including lions, leopards, cheetahs, hyenas, rhinos and giraffes, eland, buffaloes, zebras, hippos, and wildebeest. It is also home to 400 bird species. It is located only a few kilometres from the city centre.

Nairobi also has several museums. They include the National Museum of Kenya, the largest in the city.

Another major museum is the National Railway Museum, the only one of its kind in East Africa.

The city also the distinction of being home to the largest ice rink in Africa.

Other attractions in the city include Jomo Kenyatta's mausoleum, the Kenya National Theatre, the Kenya National Archives, and art galleries such as the Rahimtulla Museum of Modern Art and the Mzizi Arts Centre.

Nairobi is also known for its airport, the Jomo Kenyatta International Airport. It is the largest in East and Central Africa.

Although Nairobi is basically a modern city, with modern buildings and a good infrastructure, it is not necessarily a good place to live, especially for the majority of its residents. That is because most of them are poor. At least half of them live in slums which cover only 5 per cent of the city's total area. The city is good for people with money. That is why most wealthy Kenyans live in Nairobi.

Poverty and unemployment have contributed significantly to the high rate of crime, the highest among all the large cities in East Africa, earning Nairobi the nickname "Nairoberry." In fact, it is considered to be one of the most dangerous cities in the world.

It is also the centre of learning in Kenya with several universities and other institutions of higher learning. They include the University of Nairobi and Kenyatta University of Science and Technology.

The city of Nairobi also enjoys the unusual distinction of having the only teaching hospital in the entire East Africa, the Aga Khan Hospital which in 2005 was upgraded to that status, providing post-graduate education in medicine, surgery and nursing.

Kenyans - especially Nairobians - are also known to be more "aggressive" and more "enterprising" than their East African counterparts in Tanzania and Uganda. That is one of the main reasons, among several, the vast majority of

Tanzanians were opposed to formation of an East African political federation.

According to a survey whose results were released in 2007, about 80 percent of Tanzanians rejected fast-tracking the federation which was supposed to be consummated in 2013. The majority of the people in Tanzania believe that if the federation were formed, it would be dominated by Kenyans who would also take most of the jobs.

The people in Uganda were no more enthusiastic about the federation than their Tanzanian counterparts. Even in Kenya itself, there was very little support for the federation at the grassroots level.

Finally, East African leaders agreed at a summit in Tanzania in August 2007 that the countries involved should take a gradualist approach towards federation. The countries are Kenya, Uganda, Tanzania, and Rwanda and Burundi; the last two joined the East African Community in 2006. According to a report by Tanzanian reporter Sukhdev Chhatbar, "East African Federation: Leaders Decide Gradual Pace," in the government-owned *Daily News*, Dar es Salaam, Tanzania, 20 August 2007:

> East African Community (EAC) summit resolved here yesterday that the East African Federation (EAF) should be established gradually and step-by-step.
>
> The decision was made by the sixth extra-ordinary summit, which was attended by Presidents Yoweri Museveni of Uganda (Chairman of EAC), Mwai Kibaki of Kenya, Paul Kagame of Rwanda and host President Jakaya Kikwete. Burundi's President Pierre Nkurunziza was represented by his second deputy Vice-President Gabriel Ntisezerana.
>
> President Amani Karume attended the meeting as an observer.
>
> The EAC Secretary General, Ambassador Juma Mwapachu, told a press briefing at the end of the summit that the leaders' aim was "to build a strong and a vibrant EAF".
>
> He said that the leaders called for additional sensitization of the people on the community, including its benefits. But the summit encouraged the secretariat to further deepen regional integration.
>
> The idea of fast-tracking EAF was mooted at a summit of regional

71

presidents in 2004 and a commission under Kenya's Attorney General Amos Wako was assigned to prepare a strategic plan. The Commission had set 2013 as the year for EAF.

Mid-last year national committees were formed in partner states to collect public views on fast tracking the EAF. According to Ambassador Mwapachu, Uganda and Kenya agreed to fast tracking idea, but Tanzania overwhelmingly rejected the idea. Tanzanians opted for a gradual formation of EAF that would be led by a single president.

Ambassador Mwapachu said the leaders considered a report on the EAC position on negotiations of an EAC economic-partnership agreement with the European Union. "The summit has directed regional trade ministers and EAC ministers to meet and explore ways of negotiating as a bloc."

This, he said, was a follow up to an earlier directive issued in June, this year in Kampala.

An EAC source said that there was a broad consensus that EAC being a customs union, should negotiate as one Economic Partnership Agreement (EPA) with EU, rather than having EAC member states negotiating under different regional organizations.

According to the source, by last Sunday Tanzania, Uganda, Burundi and Rwanda were ready for EAC-EPA negotiations. Kenya, which is the current chair of the Common Market for Eastern and Southern African (COMESA), was yet to reconsider its stand.

The summit also amended treaty clauses to allow participation of Burundi and Rwanda as full members of the regional organization. Rwanda and Burundi formally joined the community in June.

With the amendments, Rwanda and Burundi each can appoint nine legislators to the EA Legislative Assembly. Each can also appoint two judges each to EA Court of Justice.

The two countries will also be represented in other organs of the Secretariat and will have to appoint deputy secretaries general.

The old EAC collapsed in 1977 because of divergent political and economic perceptions of the partner states. The new EAC was revived in 1999 and is popularised as 'people-centred'.

And according to another report from Arusha on the same subject by Adam Ihucha, "EAC Leaders Freeze Fast-Tracking Plan," in *The Guardian*, Dar es Salaam, Tanzania, 21 August 2007:

The Heads of the East African Community partner States have resolved to freeze the idea of fast-tracking the envisaged regional political federation, insisting that the gradual integration process should move along the lines of the original 'road map.'

In a joint communique read on their behalf by EAC Secretary General Juma Mwapachu at the end of their one-day summit at a tourist lodge 30 km from here yesterday, the leaders unanimously agreed that the five nations' economic, political and other links should run in phases until the ultimate goal of having a political union is achieved.

"There is a need to mobilise and deepen sensitisation on political integration and stimulate greater political will to promote deeper economic integration and lock-in gains achieved from economic cooperation," reads part of the communique from the Summit, held at the Ngurdoto Mountain Lodge.

President Yoweri Museveni of Uganda chaired the summit, which was also attended by host President Jakaya Kikwete, President Mwai Kibaki of Kenya, President Paul Kagame of Rwanda and Burundi Second Vice President Gabriel Ntisezerana.

The five leaders were also unanimous on the need to move expeditiously towards establishing a common market and a monetary union by 2012 before seeing how to have the envisaged political federation.

With their common stand coming against the backdrop of qualified support from Kenya, Uganda and Tanzania for the idea of fast-tracking the setting up of the federation, they cautioned that the road-map idea should not be undermined.

According to Mwapachu, 97 per cent of respondents in Tanzania, 76 per cent in Uganda and 70 in Kenya want political federation but have warned against its being rushed.

The Summit directed that the governments of newly admitted EAC member states, Burundi and Rwanda, undertake national consultations to gauge the people's views on the establishment of an EA political federation.

They also ordered the two countries to speed up the process of integrating fully in the EAC Customs Union.

The EAC customs union began by setting up common external tariffs for goods entering the region in January 2005 and is due to move towards a common market and a monetary union modelled on the European Union by 2012.

It was also agreed at yesterday's summit that the EAC secretariat explore the possibility of achieving the threshold of the Customs Union earlier, before developing a strategic framework for fast-tracking the establishment of a common market and a monetary union for consideration by the regional Council of Ministers and the next summit.

The summit further ordered the secretariat to quickly propose an East African Industrial and Investment strategy supported by an institutional decision-making authority, with a view to promoting equitable industrial development in the region.

With regard to the way the EAC should take in negotiating an EAC economic Partnership Agreement (EPA) with European Union as a bloc, it was resolved that modalities of doing so gainfully be devised.

The summit also endorsed amendments to some provisions in the treaty establishing the EAC as a way of facilitating the effective participation of the two new partner states in the Community's various organs and institutions.

Summit chairman Museveni said the history of humankind proved that nothing can be achieved without integration, adding that it was high time Africa faced the reality.

Economic analysts predict that businesspersons and investors in EAC member states will be whetting their appetite following the recent admission of Burundi and Rwanda into the Community.

Up for grabs will be an expanded region of 1.9 million square kilometers with a combined population of over 110 million people and a combined Gross Domestic Product of over US$41 billion.

The two countries' accession was formalised during the EAC's Fifth Extraordinary Summit in Kampala and means that, like the founding member states - Kenya, Uganda and Tanzania - Burundi and Rwanda have since this July 1 been participating in the Community's deliberations not as observers but as fully-fledged members.

This came about after the Presidents of Kenya, Uganda and Tanzania signed Treaties of Accession to the eight-year-old bloc in respect of the two new member states.

"The accession of Rwanda and Burundi to the East African Community treaty following their admission into the Community last November completes a missing link for our region," noted President Kibaki, who was also the outgoing chairman of the EAC Head of State Summit.

"The two countries are geographically, culturally and economically connected to this region, and we are therefore pleased to work closely with them in furthering the objectives of our community," he pointed out, as he handed over the chair to President Museveni after the summit.

The admission of Rwanda and Burundi into the EAC is one of the most memorable moments for EAC since President Museveni and former presidents Ali Hassan Mwinyi of Tanzania and Daniel arap Moi of Kenya reached a landmark decision in 1993 to renew regional integration by launching the East African Cooperation.

In 1999 President Museveni and former presidents Benjamin Mkapa of Tanzania and Moi signed the Treaty that transformed the East African Co-operation into the new-look East African Community, the first one having collapsed under political and other differences 30 years ago.

The Kenyan newspaper, *Daily Nation*, in its edition of 22 August 2007, had the following to say on the same subject in the editorial, "East African Leaders Got Their Priorities Right":

East African Community Heads of State meeting in Arusha this week decided to move the focus away from fast-tracking political federation.

This might, on the surface, appear like a step backwards on the march towards unity, and a victory for the naysayers in all the countries who have been rubbishing the goal of an East African Federation.

But we prefer to look at it as a pragmatic step that will help put the focus back on the basic steps that will serve as the building blocks for eventual federation.

Thus federation remains the goal; but such an ideal can only be built on putting all the little nuts and bolts in place required to hold such an entity together.

There will, for example, be need to expedite the full working of the East African Customs Union, among other steps towards economic integration.

But in addition to all the things that have to be negotiated and codified as protocol, there is much more that East African leaders can do to ensure the eventual dream is realised.

Freer movement within East Africa and fewer hindrances to normal commercial and personal contacts between the peoples are issues that can be easily resolved without a need for drawn-out negotiations. There is need to recognise that East Africans are one people, only divided by artificial borders.

All the East African leaders have talked of their support for free movement of people, labour and goods within the region, but not one of them has moved to bring down the barriers. Such are the brave gestures that would demonstrate that they are paying more than lip-service to the goal of unity.

Facilitating free movement within the region will also go a long way in helping dispel the reservations caused by baseless fears that some countries could be overshadowed by their partners.

Experience elsewhere is that it is usually the wealthy countries that fear economic and political integration because they think they will be swamped by their poorer neighbours, or be forced to prop up weaker economies.

Free movement might reveal that East Africans are far ahead of their leaders in the quest for integration.

The dominant role Nairobi has played in the history of East Africa especially when it was the headquarters of the East African Common Services Organisation (EACSO) during colonial rule has greatly contributed to the negative perception of Kenyans among their East African counterparts in Tanzania and Uganda, but especially in Tanzania, as domineering and perpetually dominant in the region.

Kenya then dominated East Africa and its entire economy. The argument is that it is going to do so again if the East African countries unite under one government. And even if it's not true, perception is reality.

One of the reasons Kenya continues to be in a dominant position among the East African countries is the level of education of its people which is comparatively high. And Nairobi continues to play a leading role as the centre for academic excellence in Kenya, hence East Africa together with Kampala (Uganda) and Dar es Salaam (Tanzania).

Next we are going to take a look at the North Eastern Province. It has a very interesting history and was once known as the Northern Frontier District during colonial rule.

The area was a centre of dispute, and armed conflict, between Kenya and Somalia n the sixties because Somalia claimed the district as part of its territory.

The province borders Somalia and is inhabited mostly by Somalis and other pastoralist communities. Its capital is Garissa and the Tana River flows through the town which is located near the Coast Province.

The Tana River is the longest river in Kenya. And one

76

of Kenya's administrative areas, Tana River District, is named after the river.

The river flows from the Aberdare Mountains to the west of Nyeri. Besides Garissa, it also passes through two other towns, Hola and Garsen, before entering the Indian Ocean. And its source, the Aberdares, are some of the most well-known mountain ranges in Africa.

The people of Garissa, like the vast majority in the North Eastern Province, would probably never have chosen to be part of Kenya had it not been for the British colonial rulers who drew the colonial boundaries in the region, separating the people from their kith-and-kin in Somalia.

The North Eastern Province covers most of northeastern Kenya and is a semi-arid region. And because of the conflict in Somalia, it has for years been a haven for refugees fleeing fighting in their home country across the border. They have mingled easily with the local population in the province because both, the refugees and the indigenous people, are mostly Somali.

The province is divided into four districts: Garissa whose capital is Garrisa which is also the provincial capital; Ijara, with Ijara as its capital; Wajir – capital Wajir; and Mandera, the capital also being known as Mandera.

Ijara is a fairly new district. It was split from Garissa. Its capital Ijara is a very remote town.

The town of Wajir is located in a drought-stricken area and has suffered severe famine through the years.

The town of Mandera has had the same fate. And the area where it is located has been the scene of clashes between Somali clans resulting in a number of deaths.

The North Eastern Province is Kenya's "forbidden" territory. And its history of conflict does little to improve its image.

Among all the conflicts which have taken place in the North Eastern Province through the years, mostly local skirmishes between different clans and tribes, one stands out as the most significant. And that was the Shifta War in the sixties when what is now the North Eastern Province was known as the Northern Frontier District.

The war is highly significant because it threatened the territorial integrity of the newly independent state of Kenya. And had the insurgents won, detaching the region from the rest of Kenya, their victory would have set a precedent on a continent where there are other people who also want to redraw the map of Africa and create new states or reunite with their kith-and-kin – members of their own tribe(s) – from whom they were separated by the colonial boundaries drawn by the imperial powers.

The Shifta War was important in another respect. It was international in character. It assumed that dimension because it involved another country, Somalia, as a party to the conflict. It also assumed an international character in another respect, although to a smaller degree as an international issue, because of the involvement of other countries – mostly African – in mediation efforts to help resolve the crisis.

Less than four days after Somalia became independent in June 1960 - former British Somaliland and Italian Somaliland united to form Somalia on attainment of sovereign status - the Somali government formally announced its desire to unite all Somali people in the Horn of Africa under one leadership and in a single political entity, creating a new bigger country for all Somalis.

Thus, the conflict acquired legitimacy and formal recognition on the part of the Somalis in Kenya and elsewhere in the region as an expression of their legitimate aspirations as a people to live under a government of their choice in pursuit of their right to self-determination.

The conflict in the Northern Frontier District was not just about land. It was, in fact, mostly about people: a determined effort by Somalis on both sides of the border to reunite, and an equally concerted effort by the Somali national government in Mogadishu, Somalia, to reunite all Somali people in neighbouring countries – including those in the Ogaden Region in Ethiopia and not just the ones in Kenya – under one government and create Greater Somalia.

About two-thirds of Somalis live in what can be described as proper Somalia, which is now a dismembered nation and disfigured by war. The rest live in Djibouti, which was once the former French Somaliland; Ethiopia, and Kenya.

And they still see themselves as one people. As Somali's first prime minister, Abdirashid Ali Shermake, bluntly stated in his refusal to accept the artificial boundaries which divided his people:

> No! Our misfortune is that our neighbouring countries, with whom we seek to promote constructive and harmonious relations, are not our neighbours but our Somali kinsmen whose citizenship has been falsified by indiscriminate boundary 'arrangements.'
> They have to move across artificial frontiers to their pasture lands. They occupy the same terrain and pursue the same pastoral economy as ourselves. We speak the same language. We share the same God, the same culture and the same traditions. How can we regard our brothers as foreigners? - Shermake, quoted by John Drysdale, *The Somali Dispute* (New York: Praeger, 1964), p. 8.

The North Eastern Province of Kenya remains a volatile region even today partly because of that, although it is not the tinderbox it once was in the sixties.

Our next trip takes us to Nyanza Province, from one extreme to the other. We have looked at the northeast, and now we are going to look at the southwest.

Nyanza Province is located in the southwestern part of Kenya on the shores of Lake Victoria. It is named after Lake Nyanza, which is the African name for Lake Victoria.

The word Nyanza means a large body of water or lake and comes from the Sukuma language, which is the language of the largest ethnic group in Tanzania, the Sukuma, whose home region borders the southern part of Lake Victoria in northern Tanzania. They virtually constitute a "nation" within a nation in terms of numbers. There are more than 3 million Sukumas, a population bigger than that of Botswana and a few other African countries.

Nyanza Province includes includes a substantial part of Lake Victoria. The largest ethnic group in the province is the Luo which is also the third largest in the country.

For many years the Luo constituted the second-largest ethnic group after the Kikuyu but have been surpassed by the Luhya in recent times.

The Luo originally came from Sudan and are Nilotic-speaking. But there are a number of Bantu-speaking tribes in Nyanza Province. They include the Kuria who are also found in neighbouring Tanzania just like the Lou are; the Gusii (Kisii), and the Luhya in much smaller numbers.

Kisumu is the provincial capital. It is also the third-largest city after Nairobi and Mombasa.

Nyanza Province was also the political stronghold of former Vice President Jaramogi Oginga Odinga, himself a Luo like the vast majority of the people in the province, just as the predominantly Kikuyu Central Province was President Jomo Kenyatta's stronghold even before he became president.

Another political luminary and Kenyatta's heir-apparent, Tom Mboya, also came from Nyanza Province and was a Luo like Oginga Odinga although they were political adversaries.

Mboya was also seen by many Kenyans to have transcended ethnicity because of his ability to mobilise forces across ethnic lines from the time when he was the nation's most prominent leader of the labour movement before independence; and his cosmopolitan outlook – he was a member of the urban elite and even represented a Nairobi constituency in parliament.

His entry into politics was facilitated by his role in the labour movement as secretary-general of the Kenya Federation of Labour (KFL); his counterpart in what was then Tanganyika was Rashidi Mfaume Kawawa who was secretary-general of the Tanganyika Federation of Labour (simply known as TFL, like KFL in Kenya) and who later became vice president of Tanganyika, later of Tanzania, under President Julius Nyerere.

Yet Mboya was always seen as a Luo by his detractors and political enemies and that cost him his life. And in spite of his profound political differences with Oginga Odinga, a Luo patriarch, his fellow tribesmen still saw him as one of their own and a distinguished son of Nyanza Province.

The politics of the province have always revolved around Kisumu because of its significance as the provincial capital and the stronghold of the predominantly Luo political elite who dominate virtually every aspect of life in this region in a country whose people mostly identify themselves on the basis of ethnicity and are divided along ethnic and regional lines.

And it is a city with an interesting history. When the port of Kisumu was founded in 1901 as the main inland terminal of the Uganda Railway, it was named Port Florence. It played a very important role as a transit point for aircraft flying from Britain to South Africa before the age of the jet airline.

The town was a landing point for passengers and mail carriers from Southampton to Cape Town. It also linked Port Bell in Uganda and Nairobi. Today, there are regular daily flights between Kisumu and Nairobi.

One of the city's best attractions is the Kisumu Museum. Established in 1980, it has a series of pavilions some of which contain live animals including crocodiles and a variety of snakes such as mambas, cobras and puff adders. Other pavilions have farming tools and artifacts made by the people of different ethnic groups in Nyanza

Province.

There is also a replica of a Luo homestead, complete with granaries and livestock corrals. The exhibition also includes traditional healing plants and explains the origin of the Luo in Sudan and their migrations from Uganda to western Kenya in the 1500s A.D.

The people of Nyanza Province, especially the Luo, were thrust into the international spotlight when a United States senator, Barack Obama, whose father was a Luo, ran for president of the United States. He entered the race in 2007 for the 2008 presidential election and was the first serious non-white contender in American history to run for president.

Nyanza Province has 12 districts. They are – with their capitals: Bondo – capital Bondo; Gucha which is also known as South Kisii District and Ogembo District whose capital is Ogembo; Homa Bay – with Homa Bay as its capital; Kisii also known as Kisii Central District whose capital is Kisii; Kisumu – capital Kisumu which is also the provincial capital; Kuria – capital Kehancha; Migori – capital Migori; Nyamira also known as North Kisii District whose capital is Nyamira; Nyando – capital Awasi; Rachuonyo – capital Oyugis; Siaya – with Siaya as its capital; and Suba District whose capital is Mbita.

The main language spoken in Nyanza Province is, of course, Luo also known as Dholuo (or Kijaluo in Kiswahili). The other languages are Gusii (Kisii), Luhya, Kuria, Kiswahili (or Swahili), and English for those who have some education, especially secondary school education and higher.

And there are other languages spoken by members of "immigrant" groups from other parts of Kenya, not indigenous to Nyanza Province.

Next we go to the Rift Valley Province. It is the largest province and one of the richest and most economically vibrant.

It borders Uganda and, as its name suggests, it is an

integral part of the Rift Valley which passes through it. The Rift Valley is its most distinctive geographical feature and a major tourist attraction.

The Rift Valley Province also has the largest population. Its capital is Nakuru.

Nakuru was founded by the British who settled in the so-called White Highlands and played an important part in the history of Kenya as a stronghold of the white settlers who did not want to relinquish control to the black African majority when the nationalist tide was sweeping across the continent during the struggle for independence in the fifties and sixties.

Agriculture, manufacturing and tourism constitute the backbone of the city's economy. There are many farms around Nakuru, large and small, where a variety of crops are grown. They include coffee, wheat, barley, maize, beans, fruits and vegetables. Dairy farming also is one of the most important activities in Nakuru and the entire province.

The town of Nakuru is also one of the most important learning centres in the country. Its institutions of higher learning include Egerton University, Kabarak University, the Rift Valley Institute of Technology, the Kenya Institute of Management, and the Kenya Industrial Training Institute. There are also a number of private colleges and secondary schools.

Tourist attractions in and around the town of Nakuru include Lake Nakuru which is a part of Nakuru National Park; Menengai Crater, a dormant volcano; and Hyrax Hill which is considered to be a major Neolithic and Iron Age site discovered by Dr. L.S.B. Leakey and his wife Mary in 1926. They found tombs and a fortress built of stone, among other findings.

Like all the other large towns and cities in Kenya, Nakuru's population is cosmopolitan with people from many parts of the world. It is predominantly black African but there is also a large number of Kenyans of Asian origin, and whites.

Another important town in Rift Valley Province is Kericho which is surrounded by highlands of fertile soil with large tea farms.

The town, and its district also called Kericho, sits at a high altitude. It gets ample rain throughout the year and is known as the centre of Kenya's large and robust tea industry.

The town is named after a Maasai chief, Ole Kericho. It is also the home town of the Kipsigis – so is Kericho District – who are a part of the Kalenjin, a collection of related ethnic groups in the Rift Valley Province.

Kericho town is also home to Africa's largest Sikh or Gurudwara place of worship.

And its economic activities are very much a reflection of the abundance the Rift Valley Province is known for throughout Kenya. Agriculture dominates the economy. But cattle raising and horticulture are also very important economic activities in the province.

The Rift Valley itself, from which the province gets its name, is an important economic resource as a major tourist attraction. It is a feature of majestic beauty, running from north to south, unparalleled in its grandeur anywhere else in the world.

It extends from Lebanon to Mozambique and divides into two, the Western Rift and the Eastern Rift, in eastern Africa. The Rift Valley Province in western Kenya is part of the Western Rift Valley.

The Western Rift also contains the Rift Valley lakes including some of the deepest in the world, such as Lake Tanganyika - south of Kenya - which is the second-deepest in the world after Lake Baikal in Russia. All the African Great Lakes (Victoria, Tanganyika, and Nyasa) were formed as a result of the rift, and most of them lie within the valley.

Lake Victoria, the second-largest freshwater lake in the world after Lake Superior in North America, actually lies

84

between the two branches of the rift – Eastern and Western Rift Valleys – but it is considered to be a part of the Rift system.

The Rift Valley Province is one of the most fertile regions, and potentially one of the richest, in the entire East Africa. And it is destined to play a critical role in Kenya's future economic development.

It can even be said that where the Rift Valley Province goes, so Kenya goes.

The province has 18 administrative districts listed here with their capitals: Baringo – capital Kabarnet; Bornet – capital Bornet; Buret – capital Litein; Kajiado – capital Kajiado; Keiyo – capital Iten/Tambach (it forms a common local authority - Iten/Tambach town council – with Tambach, a small town in the vicinity); Kericho – whose capital is also named Kericho; Koibatek – capital Eldama Ravine; Laikipia – capital Nanyuki; Marakwet – capital Kapsowar; Nakuru – Nakuru; Nandi – capital Kapsabet; Narok – capital Narok; Samburu – capital Maralal; Trans Mara – capital Kilgoris; Tans-Nzoia – capital Kitale; Turkana – capital Lodwar; Uasin Gishu – capital Eldoret; West Pokot – capital Kapenguria.

Apart from the provincial capital Nakuru, the other well-known towns in the Rift Valley Province - which are also well-known throughout Kenya and even beyond, especially in other parts of East Africa - are Eldoret, Kericho, Nanyuki, Kitale, and Naivasha.

Kapenguria is another town that is relatively well-known mainly in the history of Kenya as the town where Jomo Kenyatta and his compatriots were tried and imprisoned during Mau Mau. Their trial came to be known as the Kapnguria Trial and the town was thrust into the spotlight in the fifties because of this notoriety.

The town of Kapenguria is located northeast of Kitale, another well-known place.

Kitale is essentially an agricultural town but it is also known as one of the most diverse towns in the country.

And it is fairly large in the Kenyan context. It was founded in 1908 by the British settlers and a branch of the Uganda Railway from Eldoret reached Kitale in 1925, helping the town to grow.

The main cash crops grown around Kitale and other parts of the Trans-Nzoia District, of which Kitale is the capital, are tea, coffee, beans, maize, sunflower, and pyrethrum.

There is also a park, the Saiwa Swamp National Park, near the town of Kitale.

Another attractive feature in the area is Mount Elgon. The town of Kitale lies in the foothills of this famous mountain which is on the border of Kenya and Uganda. It is an extinct volcano, the oldest and largest solitary volcano in East Africa.

Mount Elgon is named after the Elgonyi tribe whose people once lived in huge caves on the south side of the mountain. It was known as Ol Doinyo Iigoon among the Maasai, which means "Breast Mountain." And on the Ugandan side, it was known as Masawa.

The area around the mountain is protected by two Mount Elgon National Parks. One is in Kenya and the other one in Uganda.

Eldoret is another famous town in the Rift Valley Province. It is the fastest-growing town in Kenya and the fifth-largest in the country. It is also known as a centre of learning. Moi University is the most prominent institution of higher learning in Eldoret and one of the largest in the country.

The name Eldoret comes from the Maasai word, *eldore*, which means "stony river." There is a river nearby, Sosiani River, whose bed is very stony.

The area of what is Eldoret today was first occupied by the members of the Sirikwa tribe; then by the Maasai, and the Nandi, in that chronological order, until it was finally taken over by the white settlers.

Eldoret was established in 1908 by Afrikaners who

originally came from South Africa. They "trekked" from Nakuru to Eldoret after travelling from South Africa by sea and then by train from Mombasa. Other white settlers followed shortly afterwards; so did Indians and Pakistanis, but mostly Indians, who built shops and became engaged in retail and wholesale trade.

The Ugandan Railway reached Eldoret in 1924 and was a big boost to the town in terms of economic growth. The town got another boost when Daniel arap Moi was president of Kenya. He was born in Baringo, a neighbouring district, and helped the town develop even further. And in 1984, a university was built by the government in Eldoret. It was named Moi University in honour of President Moi.

Eldoret also has a number of factories. Major industries nclude textiles, wheat, maize and pyrethrum. It is also known for the production of cheese.

Another town many people outside the Rift Valley Province know about is Naivasha. It is part of Nakuru District but is distinct in its own way. It is a small market town but a popular tourist destination and attracts many tourists to the Rift Valley Province every year.

Its tourist attractions include Hell's Gate National Park, Longonot National Park, Mount Longonot, and Lake Naivasha which has many hippos. There are many other animals in the area which draw tourists.

Its reputation as a resort town earned it distinction as the place where mediators who worked hard to end the Sudanese civil war met many times. A comprehensive peace agreement was signed between the leaders of Southern Sudan and those of the national government in Khartoum. The agreement came to be known as the Naivasha Agreement.

It is located on the shore of Lake Naivasha and along the Nairobi-Nakuru highway and the Uganda Railway. Its main industry is agriculture, especially floriculture.

Nanyuki is another well-known town in the Rift Valley

Province and throughout Kenya.

It was founded by British settlers in 1907 and is located in the central part of the country northwest of Mount Kenya. Some of the descendants of those settlers still live in Nanyuki and surrounding areas.

It is a fertile area and there are many ranches around Nanyuki. Shops in town do brisk business supplying many farms, ranches and game parks with whatever they want besides basic necessities. Originally, most of the shops in Nanyuki were owned by Indians. And they still constitute a significant part of the population.

The town also is an important tourist destination. Those who go to climb Mount Kenya pass through Nanyuki or start their expeditions from there. It is also a resting place for them. And the town has many hotels because of all this traffic. Mount Kenya Safari Club and Sportsman's Arms Hotel are the best known.

Other hotels include Lion's Court, Equatorial Hotel, Mount Kenya Paradise Hotel, and Joskaki Hotel.

The oldest restaurant in town is Marina and is still a popular spot.

Many years ago, something unique was done in Nanyuki. A restaurant was opened south of Nanyuki but was not an ordinary restaurant. It was built inside a huge tree and was named Trout Tree Restaurant.

In terms of industrial activity, Nanyuki lags far behind many other towns in Kenya. There used to be a textile factory, Nanyuki Textile Mills, but it was closed down in 1978 due to financial losses.

It was revived years later under new management and now produces some textiles.

Also saw mills which used to exist in Nanyuki have either been closed down or barely survive due to lack of lumber. Cutting down trees on Mount Kenya, which was the source of the lumber needed, is banned.

Although there isn't much industrial activity going on in Nanyuki, it is still a vibrant town and one of the most well-known in Kenya.

There is a park in the centre of the town and two rivers, Nanyuki and Liki, pass through this beautiful town. The equator also passes through the southern part of the town. It is a popular tourist spot because of this geographical distinctiveness.

Also, there are a number of parks and reserves around or near Nanyuki. They include Mount Kenya National Park, Samburu National Reserve, Sweetwaters Game Reserve, Lewa Wildlife Conservancy, and Shaba National Park.

Nanyuki also has some of the cleanest water in Kenya. It comes from a river flowing from Mount Kenya and is unpolluted.

If you go to the Rift Valley Province, Nanyuki is one of the towns you shouldn't miss. You'll never forget it, once you visit it.

From the Rift Valley Province, we finally go to the Western Province on our tour of Kenya to get a panoramic view of this region, one of the eight which collectively constitute the country's geographical and administrative units at the provincial level.

The Western Province is located west of the Eastern Rift Valley and is one of the four smallest in terms of area. The others are Nairobi Province, Nyanza Province and Central Province.

The Western Province is predominantly Luhya, a Bantu-speaking people who constitute the second-largest ethnic group after the Kikuyu.

The province is also unique in one respect. It has a very large number of Quakers, one of the largest in the world although other faiths are also practised here, including Islam, not just Christianity and traditional religion.

The Western Province is also known for its outstanding geographical features. Mount Elgon is located here, in Bungoma District which is one of the administrative units within the province. Mount Elgon is the second-highest in

Kenya after mount Kenya. And Kakamega Forest, which is a rain forest, is part of the area around Mount Elgon which is an important tourist attraction.

Kakamega Forest is said to be Kenya's last remnant of the ancient Guineo-Congolian rain forest which once spanned the continent. And the local people, the Luhya, rely heavily on the forest for their needs. The forest itself is not a tourist attraction but Mount Elgon is. But it is a region (the Western Province) which is one of the most densely-populated in Africa and perhaps in the entire world.

Kakamega is the provincial capital and the headquarters of Kakamega District. It is also one of the more well-known towns in Kenya and in neighbouring Uganda.

The area of Kakamega gets a lot of rain and includes Kakamega Forest. Kakamega is also said to be home to Africa's largest and most aggressive cobra.

The main economic activities in Kakamega are farming and fishing which provide sustenance for the Luhya more than anything else. There are also a number of companies in town, including the West Kenya Sugar Company.

There is also a new academic institution in the town of Kakamega, Masinde Muliro University of Science and Technology. It is named after a prominent national politician, Masinde Muliro, from the Western Province. It was created by an act of parliament in December 2006 and is located in the heart of Kakamega town. It is expected that the university will contribute to economic growth in the town and in the province.

Although it is relatively well-known in the country, it is not a vibrant town. The pace of life is slow, which is an attractive feature of the town for some people including visitors and tourists. But it is known in Kenyan history for one very important reason. It was the scene of the gold rush in the 1930s.

The climate of the Western Province is tropical and

varies with altitude. There are hills and mountains in the north, in Bungoma District, and lowlands in the south. The highest point is, of course, Mount Elgon; and the lowest is around Lake Victoria in Busia District in the south which borders the lake.

The town of Busia is the lowest point in the Western Province. It is located on the shores of Lake Victoria.

Kakamega District is mainly hot and wet most of the year. Bungoma is also wet but colder because of its higher altitude.

Busia District bordering Lake Victoria in the south is the warmest; the hilly Vihiga District, the coldest.

The entire Western Province experiences very heavy rainfall throughout the year. Long rains are in the earlier months of the year.

The climate has been a blessing for the province which is heavily dependent on agriculture. The northern district of Bungoma is known as sugar country. It has one of the largest sugar factories in Kenya and in the entire East Africa. There are also numerous small-holder sugar mills in the district. Maize, millet and sorghum are also grown in the district in substantial amounts. Other important economic activities in Bungoma District include dairy farming and poultry.

The district also gets a number of tourists every year, with many of them observing the cultural activities, including circumcision ceremonies, of the people in that area.

Kakamega District also is a farming area, with the people engaging in both subsistence and commercial farming. Sugar cane is the main crop. There are two sugar factories in the district and a significant tourism industry whose primary asset is the Kakamega Forest, although it is still not a major attraction.

Busia District in the south experiences perennial floods from the Nzoia River which originates from Mount Elgon flowing south and then west, and finally into Lake

Victoria near the town of Busia.

The river is very important to Western Kenya, not just to the Western Province. It flows through a region inhabited by almost 2 million people and is critical to their survival and to the region's economic development.

It provides water for irrigation throughout the year. And even the annual floods, while destructive, are a blessing to the farmers in the region. They carry fertile soil and minerals and deposit the sediment in the lowland areas, contributing significantly to agricultural production. Without the sediment washed downstream, the lowland areas would not be as fertile as they are now.

And around the industrial area at Webuye, the river absorbs a lot of effluent from the paper and sugar factories there.

Webuye is a small industrial town in Bungoma District. It is located on the main road to Uganda and is home to the Pan-African Paper Mills which is the largest paper factory in the region.

The town also has a number of heavy-chemical and sugar manufacturers. The area around Webuye is home to the Bukusu tribe.

The Nzoia River, which passes through there, also has spectacular waterfalls and great potential for generating hydroelectricity.

While Busia District is hit by floods every year from the Nzoia River, and benefits from the floods in terms of soil deposit which helps farmers in the area, the main economic activity of the people who live in the district is fishing in Lake Victoria.

There is also limited commercial farming in the area. Sugar cane is the main crop. And for subsistence farming, cassava is.

In Vihiga District are large tea plantations. The district is the most densely populated rural area in Kenya. Dairy farming is one of the most important economic activities in Vihiga. So is quarrying for construction materials.

The Western Province has many large factories. There are four sugar-processing plants. The largest is Mumias Sugar based in Mumias, a town west of Kakamega.

The province has eight districts. They are – with their capitals: Bungoma – capital Bungoma; Busia – capital Busia; Butere/Mumias – capital Butere; Kakamega – capital Kakamega; Lugari – capital Lugari; Mount Elgon – capital Kapsokwony; Teso – capital Malaba; and Vihiga – capital Vihiga.

The Western Province is well-endowed but, like in most parts of the country, the standard of living is low in this region.

The elite are the biggest beneficiaries. And most of them live in urban centres throughout Kenya, a phenomenon common across the continent and elsewhere in the Third World.

By African standards, Kenya is relatively developed. And the Western Province has the potential, in fact enormous potential, to develop like the rest of the country with the possible exception of the North Eastern Province – the former Northern Frontier District – which hardly has anything in terms of natural resources besides the people themselves.

But that is an entirely different subject beyond the scope of this work.

Chapter Five:

The People of Kenya: An Ethnic Profile

KENYA has people of all races but the vast majority of them are members of indigenous groups. They are black African.

Although there are significant numbers of Kenyans of Asian, Arab and European origin, they are vastly outnumbered by the members of black African tribes or ethnic groups.

The main non-indigenous groups are Gujaratis, Punjabis and Goans from India; Arabs mostly from Oman; and the British. Although they are not black, they are also African since Africa is their home.

Kenyan Professor Ali Mazrui classifies non-indigenous people in Africa as Africans of the soil, as opposed to black Africans whom he calls Africans of the blood.

There are basically 42 black African ethnic groups or tribes in Kenya.. But the number goes up to 49 depending on who defines them.

Some of them are related and are so close that they are not considered to be separate tribes.

All 49 are listed here in alphabetical order:

Ameru, Bajuni, Bukusu, Choyi, Digo, Duruma, Elgeyo, Embu, Giryama, Isukha, Jibana, Kalenjin, Kamba, Kambe,

Kauma, Kikuyu, Kipsigis, Kissi, Kore, Kuria, Luhya, Luo, Maasai, Maragoli, Marakwet, Marama, Miji Kenda, Nandi, Ogiek, Orma, Oromo, Pokomo, Pokot, Rabai, Rendille, Ribe, Sabaot, Samburu, Sengwer, Somali, Suba, Swahili, Tachoni, Taita, Taveta, Terik, Tugen, Turkana, Yaaku.

Together with the five non-black groups we mentioned earlier – the Gujaratis, Punjabis, Goans, Arabs, and Britons – Kenya has 53 ethnic groups.

We are going to take a closer look at some of them to get a better understanding of the ethnic composition of this East African country.

Black African ethnic groups in Kenya are divided into three linguistic categories: Bantu, Nilotic, and Cushite. The Bantu constitute the majority. They include the Kikuyu, the Kamba, and the Luhya who are also among the five largest ethnic groups in the country.

The Kikuyu, the Luhya, the Kamba, the Meru, the Embu and the Gusii (Kisii) constitute the majority of the Bantu in Kenya. And they are mostly farmers like most Bantus are. But many of them also own cattle.

The Kikuyu homeland is around Mount Kenya and it is believed they arrived in the area in the 1700s.

There are many theories concerning their origin. Some say they migrated from Mozambique; others say from Congo.

What is clear from archaelogical and linguistic evidence is that they arrived in East Africa about 2,000 years ago from West Africa, especially from the Nigeria/Cameroon border area, as did the rest of the Bantu-speaking people, and their language belongs to the Niger-Congo family.

They have interacted with their neighbours, the Maasai, for a long time. The Maasai usually raided the Kikuyu for cattle and women, and the Kikuyu fought back. But in spite of all that, the two groups built strong commercial ties through the years and their people have been intermarrying almost from the time they first came into contact with each other in central Kenya.

Another major Bantu ethnic group, the Kamba, also has an interesting history. It is said the Kamba migrated from what is now western Tanzania, a region occupied by the Nyamwezi ethnic group, one of the largest in Tanzania; implying that they were part of the Nyamwezi or are related to them. They moved east to the Usambara Mountains in northeastern Tanzania and eventually found their way to a semi-arid region in eastern Kenya which became their new home.

Other researchers contend that the Kamba are a product of many ethnic groups who intermarried and ended up creating a new ethnic group.

Whatever the case, it is generally believed that they arrived in their present homeland east of Nairobi towards the Tsavo National Park about 200 years ago.

The Kamba today are one of the most successful groups in Kenya, and one of the most well-known in East Africa.

In the past, they had a reputation as excellent traders, carrying on trade from the coast all the way to Lake Victoria, and all the way up to Lake Turkana. They traded in ivory, honey, weapons, beer, and ornaments.

They also excelled in barter, exchanging goods for food with their neighbours: the Maasai and the Kikuyu. It was a matter of survival. They could not always produce much since their home region was arid or semi-arid land, forcing them to find food elsewhere.

And during colonial rule, the British "respected" them for their intelligence. They also had a reputation as fighters, another quality the British liked since they could use them as soldiers and as policemen. Many Kambas were conscripted into the army and fought in both world wars.

Even today, many Kambas serve in the armed forces and in law enforcement.

The Luhya are another major Bantu ethnic group in Kenya. Although successful, they have had to contend with problems of high population density through the years in a region where there is not enough fertile land for all the people.

The Meru and the Embu are the other Bantu ethnic groups in Kenya. They are related to the Kikuyu and are essentially farmers. They grow coffee, tea, maize, potatoes and pyrethrum as well as other crops. The Embu are also well-known for their honey and for dancing on stilts.

Then there are the Nilotic-speaking people as a major linguistic category in Kenya besides the Bantu.

The Nilotic group includes the Luo, the third largest ethnic group in the country. Other Nilotic-speaking groups include the Maasai, the Turkana, the Samburu, and the Kalenjin.

Originally, the Luo were pastoralists. But they changed their way of life when rinderpest killed their cows and they became farmers and fishermen. Their involvement in fishing was facilitated by their geographical proximity to Lake Victoria in their new home region after they migrated from Sudan via Uganda. Some of them came straight from Sudan.

Like the Kikuyu, the Luo also played a major role in the struggle for independence. Some of the most prominent Luo politicians of national and international statures include former Vice President Oginga Odinga, Minister of Economic Planning Tom Mboya, Foreign Affairs Minister Dr. Robert Ouko, and independence leader Achieng Oneko.

And the most prominent Luo outside Kenya and Africa is United States Senator Barack Obama of Illinois. His father, also named Barack Obama after whom the son was named, earned a Ph.D. in economic from Harvard University and returned to Kenya where he served under President Jomo Kenyatta. He died in a car accident in Kenya in 1980.

He was one of the hundreds of Kenyan students who went to school in the United States on scholarships on the famous Tom Mboya Airlift in 1959.

Another Nilotic group, the Kalenjin, has an interesting history in terms of identity. The Kalenjins are actually a collection of related ethnic groups who speak the same language. They include the Kipsigis, renowned worldwide as long-distance runners; the Nandi, the Tugen and the Elyogo. President Daniel arap Moi was a Tugen.

The Kalenjin were once mainly pastoralists like the vast majority of the Nilotic-speaking people. And many of them still are today. But they are also engaged in agriculture in their fertile home region, the Rift Valley Province.

Besides the Luo, the most well-known Nilotic-speaking Kenyans are the Maasai, followed by the Turkana and the Samburu. The Maasai, who also came from Sudan like other Nilotic-speaking peoples in Kenya, Tanzania and Uganda, are a small minority in both Kenya and Tanzania but are known worldwide because of their lifestyle and reputation as warriors.

They are also fiercely proud of their culture and way of life and have strongly resisted external pressure – including pressure from some national leaders – to change and adapt to "modern" ways, which is a euphemism for the "Western" way of life.

They own not only cows but also goats. But cows are their most important possession in their social, political and economic life.

There are two ethnic groups closely related to the Maasai: the Samburu and Turkana.

The traditional homeland of the Samburu is around Maralal in northern-central Kenya, an arid region. Like the Maasai, they also have the *morani*, the young warriors; also like the Maasai, they prefer red blankets and use red ochre to paint their heads.

The women wear beads. And like the Maasai, they also

own cows and goats, with the cows being their most important possession and the centre of their social, political and economic life.

Unlike some Nilotic-speaking people who have adopted other ways of life to adjust to new realities, the Samburu have remained pastoralist, preferring a nomadic way of life. When pasture becomes scarce in their arid and semi-arid homeland, they pack up and go, taking their *manyata* (portable houses and other essential items) on their camels to find better pastures. This is similar to what Somalis do. But they are not related. The Somali are Cushitic.

The other major Nilotic-speaking group is the Turkana. The Turkana have a reputation as fierce fighters, just like their kith-and-kin the Maasai and the Samburu. They own other animals besides cows. They have goats, sheep, and camels, but cow ownership is still the most important aspect of their social, political and economic life. They live in an arid region near Lake Turkana.

And all three – the Maasai, the Samburu and the Turkana – are cattle rustlers. The government has not been able to stop them and law enforcement officials usually leave them alone.

Disputes among them are settled by their elders. They were colonised like the rest of the Africans but the colonial rulers failed to conquer them in one fundamental respect: their way of life which has remained intact for hundreds of years.

The other major linguistic group is the Cushitic. The Cushites are a minority in Kenya and live mostly in the North Eastern Province which borders Somalia and Ethiopia. They include the Somali, the Boran, the El Molo, the Burji Dassenich, the Gabbra, the Orma, the Sakuye, the Boni, the Wata, the Yaaka, the Daholo, the Rendille, and the Galla.

The Somali and the Galla are the most well-known. But it is the Somali who are the dominant group in the region.

They own cattle, goats, sheep, and camels in the arid and inhospitable region of northern Kenya and lead a nomadic way of life in search of water and pasture for their herds. They also have a reputation as fierce fighters.

Another group is the Swahili. They are some of the most well-known people in East Africa, especially in Kenya and Tanzania, but they don't constitute an ethnic group the way the Kikuyu or the Luo do. They are essentially a linguistic and cultural group, and a product of many tribes and non-indigenous groups especially the Arabs. They live mostly along the coast.

Also most of the Arabs live along the coast. They are one of the three main non-indigenous groups in Kenya, the other ones being Asian and British.

Most Arabs speak Swahili and see themselves as Africans, not as citizens of the Arab world. Most Arabs in Kenya are Kenyan citizens.

There are also many Arabs in Kenya who are not Kenyans. They come mainly from Yemen and are small traders. They are commonly known as *Washihiri* or simply *Shihiri*, but mostly as *Washihiri* in Kiswahili; a term also applied to them in neighbouring Tanzania.

The British are also a significant minority and Kenya has one of the largest European communities in Africa. Kenyans of British descent include members of the aristocracy. And many of them continue to have great influence in the country especially among the elite including national leaders.

Kenyans of Asian descent, commonly known as Indians, are the most prosperous group in Kenya – and the rest of East Africa – besides the British and other whites who have always been on top.

The term "Indian" is collectively used to identify Pakistanis as well, although the majority of the Asians in Kenya came from India.

India and Pakistan were one country until 1947 and most of the immigrants in East Africa today immigrated to

100

the region before Indian independence in 1947 when the sub-continent was split into India and Pakistan.

So, in a way, the term "Indian" is the appropriate designation even for those who came from Pakistan. They all came from the Indian sub-continent as a geographical entity.

The prosperity of Indians in Kenya and other parts of Africa has been a source of resentment towards them among many black Africans. But the resentment is also attributed to the mistreatment of the indigenous people whom the majority of Indians see as inferior to them.

It is raw-naked racism even if one may argue that they are clannish more than anything else. Indians are both clannish and racist; a fact acknowledged even by some Indians themselves who admit that black Africans are exploited and mistreated by them.

And social interaction between the two as equals is almost totally out of the question. It is also extremely rare for black Africans and Indians to intermarry. Where such unions have taken place, mostly illicit relationships, it has been between Indian men and black African women. Black men dating Indian girls or women, let alone marrying them, is considered taboo by most Indians, although there have been a number cases where this taboo has been broken especially in recent times.

Marriage within the "clan," that is, within the Indian or Asian community as it is also called, is strictly enforced almost with religious zeal and devotion. And anyone who defies that risks ostracisation.

However, many Indians are tolerant of marriage with whites – and even accept it whether or not it involves Indian women and white men. The biggest concern has been about non-Indians, especially blacks, dating or marrying Indian women.

The willingness of Indians to accept unions between whites and Indians has only reinforced the belief and vindicated the claim of those who say Asians are racist towards blacks more than anybody else.

In spite of the poor race relations between Indians and black Africans in Kenya and other African countries, there is no question that the vast majority of Indians consider Africa to be home.

This was clearly demonstrated in the late sixties and in the seventies when many Indians left Tanzania and Kenya for India with the intention of living there permanently. They said they were returning to their homeland. And they did in large numbers.

But they couldn't fit in and returned to East Africa despite the fact that India was their ancestral homeland. That is because they were African more than anything else. India was the home of their ancestors, not theirs. They were born and brought up in East Africa, as were their parents and grandparents in many cases, and were therefore East Africans, not Indians of India.

After looking at the major ethnic and linguistic groups in the country, we now turn our attention to some of the other groups which are numerically smaller but no less important as an integral part of Kenya.

The Bajuni are among those groups. They are a small ethnic group in the Coast Province. They live mostly in northern Kenya. Some of them also live in southern Somalia. And they are mostly fishermen and sailors. But they are also involved in other economic activities including metalwork. They speak a language which is basically Kiswahili, or Swahili, although they call their version Kibajuni.

The word Kibajuni is also a Kiswahili term. Ki- is a prefix in Kiswahili applied to all languages. Thus, the Kikuyu speak Kikuyu, the Kamba, Kikamba, and the Luo, Kiluo. It goes on and on.

The Bajuni call themselves and are known as Wabajuni; which is another Swahili or Kiswahili term. Wa- is a prefix denoting collective identity. The Kikuyu are called Wakikuyu in Kiswahili; the Meru are called

Wameru; the Somali are called Wasomali; and Swahili are called Waswahili.

Then there are the Bukusu among the smaller groups. They don't constitute a distinct ethnic entity but are a sub-ethnic group of the Luhya. There are 17 such sub-groups which collectively constitute the Luhya ethnic group.

The Bukusu are therefore an example of many other groups in Kenya which are not considered by some people to be tribes or separate ethnic groups but sub-tribes. But they are the largest sub-group in the Luhya ethnic entity which some people call the Luhya "nation."

The Luhya is called a "nation" - mostly by the Luhya themselves - mainly because of its size; the same thing which could be applied to other large ethnic groups such as the Kikuyu, the Luo and the Kamba.

The Nandi, although a sub-group of the Kalenjin, are considered to be a separate tribe just like the other Kalenjin sub-groups – the Turkana and the Kipsigis. They live mostly in the highland areas of the Nandi Hills in the Rift Valley Province and have a reputation as fierce fighters like their brethren, the other Kalenjins. They are farmers and cattle-herders.

The Pokot are also Kalenjin but a distinct group. They live in West Pokot District and Baringo District. They are found in eastern Uganda in Karamoja District. They also have a reputation as fierce fighters as most Nilotic-speaking tribes do. They are both farmers and pastoralists, usually depending on where they live. The Hill Pokot live in the highlands and are farmers; while the Plains Pokot in the dry and infertile plains own livestock – cattle, sheep, and goats.

The Gusii, also known as Kisii, are Bantu and live in Kisii (Gusii) District in Nyanza Province in western Kenya whose dominant group is the Nilotic Luo.

They are isolated as a Bantu group in the sense that they are surrounded by Nilotic-speaking tribes – the Luo, the Maasai, the Kipsigis, and the Nandi – who traditionally have been hostile towards them. As a result, they became tough fighters themselves in order to be able to defend themselves against the Nilotic cattle raiders.

The Kisii live in a very fertile hilly district where they grow a lot of tea, coffee, bananas and other crops. But there is shortage of land and many Kisii have migrated to other parts of Kenya.

The Kisii are also one of the largest ethnic groups in Kenya. They rank fifth after the Kamba who are preceded by the Kikuyu, the Luhya, and the Luo.

All the largest ethnic groups in Kenya are Bantu – Kikuyu, Luhya, Kamba, and Kisii – except the Luo who rank third; they used to be second until they were surpassed by the Luhya.

The Kuria straddle the Kenyan-Tanzanian border close to Lake Victoria. They are found in Mara Region in northern Tanzania – which is also the home region of former Tanzanian President Julius Nyerere who was a member of the Zanaki tribe in Musoma District, Mara Region – and in Nyanza Province.

The Digo are another ethnic group found in both Kenya and Tanzania. They are a Bantu group and live along the coast in both countries between Mombasa in southern Kenya and Tanga in northern Tanzania. The majority of them live in Kenya.

The Orma live in southeastern Kenya mostly along the lower Tana River. They are also called Galla, a term commonly used in Ethiopia to identify the same ethnic group.

They are semi-nomadic and move from their southeastern desert homes only during the rainy season when they go inland in search of pastures for their livestock.

The Oromo are found mostly in Ethiopia but also in Kenya and Somalia in smaller numbers. In fact, they are the largest ethnic group in Ethiopia. They are Cushitic.

They are also one of the largest Cushitic-speaking

ethnic groups in Eastern and Northeastern Africa which includes the Horn of Africa. And their physical features, and language as well as culture, clearly distinguishes them from Bantu and Nilotic groups in Kenya, pointing to their "origin" in the Horn of Africa. The Orma or Galla are related to them.

The Pokomo are a Bantu group who live along the Tana River in the Tana River District and are mostly farmers.

The Rendille are one of the groups which are considered to be on the verge of extinction unless something is done to save them from this catastrophe.

They are nomadic pastoralists and live in the Kaisut Desert. in Northern Kenya where they roam on their camels with their livestock which is their main source of sustenance. Meat and milk are a main part of their diet.

Another group that is considered to be a part of another tribe yet is distinct from that tribe and has its own identity is the Samburu whom we earlier briefly looked at.

They are related to the Maasai. And they call themselves Lokop or Loikop. And they speak the Samburu language, not Maasai.

But like the Maasai, they are part of the Maa-speaking people. And about 95 per cent of the words of both languages – Samburu and Maasai – are the same, showing that they are indeed basically the same people.

In fact, even the name Samburu is of Maasai origin and comes from the word *samburi* which is a leather bag used by the Samburu to carry a variety of items. But, for whatever reason, they acquired their own ethnic identity. Some people have attributed this to the colonial rulers who sometimes divided people to "create" different ethnic groups for administrative purposes and to facilitate colonial rule.

They are also said to have multiple origins, although all related. Some Samburu are descended from the Maasai, and others from the Turkana, Borana (also called Boran), and Rendille. And all these are Nilotic groups.

Although they own mainly cattle, they also have sheep, goats and camels as an important part of their livestock in an arid region which forces them to have a large number of animals many of which don't survive because of the harsh climate.

Samburu District was once a large part of the Northern Frontier District (NFD) - as the region was called before and a few years after independence - which is now the North Eastern Province. It was isolated for all practical purposes and only government officials were allowed to enter the region.

It was closed to foreigners and one had to get special permission to enter the Northern Frontier District. Even today, Samburu District is a remote, harsh area.

Like the Maasai, the Samburu also came from Sudan. And they are more conservative – much more traditional in life and attitude – than their cousins the Maasai; which is quite a distinction since the Maasai themselves have quite a reputation for resisting alien influences. And they are equally proud of such stiff resistance.

Another small tribe is the Taveta. The Taveta are a Bantu ethnic group who live in south-central Kenya. They are called Wataveta in Kiswahili, and call themselves that, and their language – also in Kiswahili – is known as Kitaveta.

There are also elements of other tribes in the Tavetan population, especially the Taita, the Kamba, the Maasai, and the Chaga. The Chaga are a tribe in northeastern Tanzania in Kilimanjaro Region on the southern and southeastern slopes of Mount Kilimanjaro and throughout Moshi District.

The Taveta live mostly between Tsavo National Park and the Tanzanian border and are mostly subsistence farmers. Some of them also work on local sisal plantations and are engaged in other economic activities.

Then there are the Yaaku. They are of Cushitic origin

but gave up their original language and now speak a Maasai variant known as Mukogodo-Maasai. They were assimilated by the Maasai but some words from their old Yaaku language are a part of their vocabulary today.

They live in the Mukogodo forest west of Mount Kenya, which is a division of the Laikipia District in the Rift Valley Province, and were once hunter-gatherers and bee-keepers. They eventually adopted the Maasai pastoralist culture, although some of them are still bee-keepers.

They now consider themselves to be a sub-tribe of the Maasai, and are indeed Maasai in terms of language and culture. All the old people who spoke the original Yaaku language are dead.

Tragically, the Yaaku are some of the people who have lost their original language and culture due to assimilation, a fate that has befallen other indigenous groups in different parts of the world with dire consequences: loss of identity, turning them into carbon copies, poor carbon copies, of other people.

It is a tragic loss.

Chapter Six:

The Traditional Way of Life: A Look at African Cultures

A FUSION of cultures through the centuries has produced a synthesis that is uniquely Kenyan. And it is the local component – African tribes and their cultures found only in Kenya – that has given this cultural blend or amalgam its unique character.

It has been a confluence of cultures, flowing for centuries from Asia and the Middle East, and later from Europe, mingling with African cultures not only in Kenya but in other parts of East Africa, especially neighbouring Tanzania. And it has been one of the most exciting events, and one of the most enriching experiences, in the history of human interaction.

But while all these foreign cultures spread to other parts of the region besides Kenya, during the same period, they did not produce exactly the same synthesis when they fused with local cultures because the tribes found in Tanzania, for example, are not the same tribes that are found in Kenya except a few like the Maasai and the Digo found in both countries; and the Luo found in Kenya, Uganda and Tanzania.

Each of these cultural and linguistic groups found in

108

Kenya has its own way of life that has persisted through the centuries. Some of these groups form clusters. And it is these groups and their different ways of life which we are going to focus on in this chapter to get some understanding of the African way of life in this East African country.

Some of the most fascinating cultures have evolved in the mountainous regions of Kenya and geography has had a profound influence on their evolution:

(A) diversity of cultures (in Africa)...evolved through the centuries as a result of migrations which necessitated adaptation to new environments. Such evolution of cultures and customs also reflects the nature of the new environments including geography. For example, Mount Kenya would not have figured prominently in Kikuyu customs had there been no Mount Kenya in the area where the Kikuyu settled. - (Godfrey Mwakikagile, *Africa and The West* (Huntington, New York: Nova Science Publishers, Inc.,), p. 12).

It means the Kikuyu would have found another point of reference or a geographical feature of cultural relevance and religious significance – based on their beliefs – had there been no such mountain.

It could have been a lake, a valley, or even a desert, and would still have served the same purpose as Mount Kenya does today as the home of the Kikuyu god, *Ngai*, and which they face when they pray as Jomo Kenyatta eloquently stated in his study of Kikuyu culture, customs and beliefs appropriately entitled, *Facing Mount Kenya* first published in 1938.

According to Kikuyu beliefs, all creation began at the summit of Mount Kenya. The snow-capped peak of the mountain is the creator's dwelling place.

The Kikuyu believe that *Ngai*, whom they say is the supreme creator, came down from the heavens to his mountainous throne to survey his newly created lands. The mountain became *Kirinyaga*, his resting place, and it was from here that he called forth Gikuyu, the father of the

Kikuyu people.

It is a rough equivalent of the Biblical account of creation and the Kikuyu may or may not have appropriated some concepts from the Bible and incorporated them into their beliefs through the years, although this is highly unlikely since they had their own system of belief, already well-established, long before Christianity was introduced to them.

The Kikuyu believe *Ngai* told Gikuyu, the father of the Kikuyu people, or the Kikuyu nation, that all the lands around Kirinyaga would be the home of Gikuyu and his children forever.

The Kikuyu belief in *Ngai* as their creator also says that *Ngai* sent Gikuyu to a grove of fig trees where he found a woman called Mumbi who became his wife.

The grove of fig trees came to be known as *Mukuru wa Nyagathanga*, which means the birthplace of all Kikuyus. And it is still revered by the Kikuyu today as a sacred place and as an integral part of their very being, heart and soul.

The Kikuyu also sacrifice a goat beneath a fig tree as an offering to their god, *Ngai*, in times of drought when they pray for rain.

When the Kikuyu migrated to the central highlands of Kenya, they came into contact with the Maasai with whom they shared some traditional practices including the way they dressed, in some respects. A lot of intermarriage between the members of the two tribes also took place.

The intermarriage led to the integration of some Maasai clans into the Kikuyu nation of which they became an integral part indistinguishable from the Kikuyu themselves. It was total integration and assimilation, and the dominant culture after this absorption of the Maasai took place was Kikuyu.

Although some elements of foreign cultures have become a part of the Kikuyu way of life, for example Western civilisation, there is still a very strong sense of commitment to the traditional way of life - in terms of values - among many Kikuyus including educated ones. And they have always remained bound by strict and strong ties of clan loyalty and an even stronger sense of tribal unity traced all the way back to the time when their nation came into being. This is a very important part of Kikuyu culture.

Unfortunately, it also fosters tribalism in a heterogeneous society like Kenya. And that is one of the main reasons tribalism is so entrenched in this country of about 50 ethnic groups. And as the dominant tribe in Kenya, the Kikuyu have played a prominent role in sustaining tribalism across the spectrum.

Yet, it can also be explained in terms of their culture and origin as a people who are supposed to stick together and who see themselves as one, with a common ancestry, descended from Gikuyu and Mumbi, their original parents.

They all belong to one family, *Nyumba ya Mumbi*, which literally means the house of Mumbi who was the mother of the Kikuyu nation. And the house was established by the couple that was the progenitor of the Kikuyu nation.

The Kikuyu have nine clans and their society is strongly patriarchal. And traditional ceremonies involving rites of passage – initiation and marriage – are a very important part of the Kikuyu way of life even among urban dwellers, although there are those who may shun them and see them as "primitive" and "backward" practices.

Besides Mount Kenya and its cultural and religious significance for the Kikuyu, another important mountain in the country is Mount Elgon.

It also has important cultural and historical significance for the people who live around it.

Long before Europeans came, the mountain had deep caves in which herds of cattle could be hidden and protected. Great piles of grain were also stored in the caves.

The original inhabitants around this area looked like the Maasai in terms of physical appearance. In fact, for a long time, many people thought they were indeed Maasai. But they were not.

They were members of four very small tribes known as the Kony, the Sapei, the Pok, and the Bungomek. They are still there today and are collectively known as the Saboat. They are a part of the Kalenjin, which itself is a collection of related tribes.

There is a strong cultural affinity among the Kalenjin and the Saboat have the strongest ties with the Nandi in terms of culture.

The Saboat called the mountain, Masop, and made excellent use of this mountainous area. It was perfect for their needs. They grew crops on the mountain slopes, and they also had livestock, especially cows.

They knew about the caves in what is now called Mount Elgon and used them as granaries and stables for their livestock. The caves were also an excellent place of refuge for the Saboat during inter-tribal wars. They also protected them from bad weather.

Mount Elgon also provided them with much-needed salt. The salt was in the caves. Elephants would make trips to the caves every night to scrape the walls with their tasks and lick the salt which fell to the ground. Then the Saboat would go to the caves to collect some of the salt after the elephants were gone and use it to preserve their food.

Hunting was also common in Saboat culture. Even elephants were hunted. The Saboat used pit traps at the entrance of the caves to catch them.

Besides the Saboat, there is another group of people, the Teso, to whom Mount Elgon is very important.

They come from the Karamajong region in Uganda. No one is exactly sure if they are descended from the Karamajong, a Ugandan tribe, but they do have strong cultural and linguistic ties to the region which includes

Mount Elgon in this border area where Kenya and Uganda share a common boundary.

They have been influenced by neighbouring tribes through the years, absorbing some of their cultural elements and practices. Some of the people who have influenced them are the Luo but they have closest ties with the Pokot, a Kalenjin tribe found throughout western Laikipia and the area north of the Cherangani Hills.

It is these cultural ties between the Pokot and the Teso which separate the Pokot - or distinguishes them - from the rest of the Kalenjin tribes. But there is one major difference between the two groups.

For a long time, the Pokot have had two distinct tribal units: nomadic cattle herders and farmers. By remarkable contrast, the Teso were originally farmers who recently became cattle herders.

The culture of the Teso is defined by its age system, and respect for elders is extremely important as it is in all African cultures. Traditionally, power in a Teso clan and in the tribe itself comes from seniority. It is vested in older people.

Initiation is also a very important part of Teso culture but traditionally it was not through circumcision – a practice the Teso adopted from the Karamajong – but through animal sacrifice and big feasts that young men were initiated into manhood.

The Teso also had a strong belief in divining and prophecy and it is still a very important part of their culture even today.

Traditional diviners, called *emuron*, cast sandals on the ground and, depending on how they fall, read their positions to tell the future and detect signs for things to come. It is also a common religious practice in the traditional beliefs of other northern Kenyan tribes such as the Pokot, the Samburu, and the Borana (or Boran).

With its location on the Kenyan-Ugandan border, Mount Elgon serves as some sort of "cultural" bond between the tribes on both sides of the border which share many cultural traits.

Both the Saboat in Kenya and the Teso in Uganda have many bonds and cultural ties to Eastern Ugandan tribes, and Mount Elgon has figured prominently in their history. The boundary between the two countries has done little to sever those ties

Roughly in the same region are the Western Highlands. It is an area of great cultural significance and the highlands once served as a meeting point for two ethnic groups.

The area was originally inhabited by a Cushitic people who migrated from southern Ethiopia. Then came Nilotic tribes from southern Sudan and Uganda who settled in the same region. The result was intermarriage between these two groups, producing a synthesis of cultures we see today.

The cultures which evolved in these highlands, with their Nilotic and Cushitic content, remain separate from other Nilotic – Maasai, Samburu, and Luo – and Cushitic cultures. The other Cushitic cultures referred to here which are separate from the Cushitic cultures in the highlands include the Gabbra, and Boran Oromo.

The ones in the Western Highlands are distinct from them despite their common origin because of the cultural amalgamation that took place in those highlands between Nilotic and Cushitic cultures.

The cultures of the Western Highlands are sometimes identified as Highland Nilotes. The common name is Kalenjin.

The Kalenjin are united by a strong sense of community and rites of passage. This is a very important aspect of their culture. There is also a common belief among them in the not-so-distant past which said children were not members of the tribe. They became members only after they had been initiated.

One of the more well-known and bigger Kalenjin

groups is the Kipsigis. Traditionally, they had an elaborate and extensive system of clans, and were socially centred around a unit called the *kokuet*.

It was a large collection of up to 60 family homesteads and was structured as an insurance and support unit, not just for economic needs but for social needs as well, including emotional support and other kinds of support across a wide range of spectrum.

The families relied on each other for support and assistance in times of need. And they still do so today in this deeply conservative society proud of its resistance to change and foreign influences.

The tribe which the Kipsigis are closely related to is the Nandi.

The traditional homeland of the Nandi was the Kapsabet region, while that of the Kipsigis was the area of Kericho where these former cattle herders turned to agriculture throughout the 20th century, growing tea and other crops, as they still do today. And both tribes live in the same areas as their traditional strongholds.

The social structure of the Nandi was and still is very similar to that of the Kipsigis. The collective homesteads of the Nandi are called *pororiet*.

Initiation has always been an important part of Nandi culture which is characterised by an age-set system. Young men who became warriors were initiated at a ceremony where a white bull was sacrificed, and much of the same practice goes on today.

The Nandi have always been great cattle raiders. Historically, they raided the Luo and the Maasai. They also attacked caravans of traders from the coast who went far into the interior to conduct business.

Their reputation as fierce fighters was enhanced when they took on the British who entered their territory in the early part of the 20th century. British forces were repeatedly repelled by Nandi warriors.

It was not until after a five-year military campaign by

British forces that the Nandi were finally subdued. But they went down in history with their reputation as fighters intact, despite losing the war.

The Nandi generally maintained cordial relations with the other Kalenjin groups with whom they shared cultural affinity. They included the Elgeyo and the Tugen who have always had a reputation as great farmers.

Among the crops grown in the region were maize and millet, as they still are today. The tribes in the region also kept large herds of cattle, goats and sheep as they still do today.

Another Kalenjin tribe was the Marakwet living on Cherengani Hills. They shared many cultural traits with the other Kalenjin groups in the region. The Marakwet were made up of six clans. The name Cherengani for the hills comes from the name of one of the clans.

The Marakwet built terraced villages on the slopes of the hills, as they still do today, and goats remain the most common and most important animal members of this tribe like to keep for one very important reason: the goats are well adapted to life on the steep slopes of the Cherengani Hills.

Further south are the Kisii who probably migrated from Uganda. Unlike the rest of the people in the region, they are a Bantu group, therefore have a Bantu culture and share many cultural elements with other Bantu cultures.

When the Luo, a Nilotic group, migrated to the region from Sudan in the mid-500s, the Kisiis were forced to relocate.

Raids on the Kisii by the Maasai and the Kipsigis, both Nilotic like the Luo, also forced the Kisii to find a new home in the highlands where they continued to live as farmers. Even today, the highlands are considered to be their homeland. And their culture has evolved to suit the environment.

The Kisii have a reputation as great farmers and through the years have traded with the Luo, selling their agricultural products to them. The interaction has also led to an accommodation of cultures, and with some cultural elements flowing from both sides influencing each other in varying degrees.

Some of the most outstanding products of Kisii culture include wooden stools and different items of furniture. The Kisii, who have quite a reputation as excellent craftsmen in addition to their reputation as great farmers, also quarry and carve soapstone.

Another area of Kenya whose hills and mountains are inextricably linked with the culture of the people who live there is in the southern part of the country. It is the region of the Taita and Chyulu Hills, framing the vast plains of Tsavo and lying within view of Mount Kilimanjaro in neighbouring Tanzania.

The Chyulu hills form a border between the plains of Amboseli and the wilderness of Tsavo. This is also border country between Maasailand and Kambaland. And members of both tribes – the Maasai and the Kamba – are found throughout the area.

The Maasai graze their herds in this area. It is also here where the Kamba crossed the hills a long time ago when they migrated from the Usambara mountains in northeastern Tanzania after their long journey from what is now western Tanzania, their original homeland.

And both tribes share a common belief about the existence of *Shetani*, which means Satan or the Devil in Kiswahili, in the area. Many local people say the area is haunted by the ghosts of the people who died and got buried under the lava of these hills. A large lava flow took place in this area a long time ago and claimed many lives, according to local legend.

Many people in the area claim that mournful cries can be heard from under the ground at night, and have been known to leave offerings of food on the rocks to appease the departed souls trapped there.

The Taita Hills are the homeland of the Taita people.

They are a well-established tribe in the region and are believed to have migrated from the northeastern coast of Kenya.

During their long occupancy of the Taita Hills, they have developed a strong and unifying cultural character and the hills are very much an integral part of their lives, hence their culture.

The Taita are also some of Kenya's best farmers and are known as a strongly agricultural people. They have a long history of well-developed agriculture and have for years grown millet and sugar cane. They later started growing maize.

They also built highly developed systems of irrigation using hollowed sugar cane pipes. Water was transported fairly long distances, sometimes for about a mile. Cultivation entailed extensive clearance of land, with men clearing the land, and women cultivating and working the fields. That is how it was traditionally done according to their culture. And they still do it today.

They did not keep animals except only on a limited scale, and cow ownership is a relatively new practice among them. They started acquiring cattle only in the 20th century. But they were highly skilled in using iron, making agricultural implements and weapons.

The Taita had six traditional clans, named numerically in the order by which each group were believed to have migrated to the hills from northeastern Kenya.

Inter-clan ties were not particularly strong but they shared traditional customs which were unified, thus forming some kind of indissoluble bonds among them.

Some of the caves in the Taita Hills have great cultural and religious significance. They are considered to be sacred and were used as a repository for ancestral skulls in keeping with their traditional religion of ancestor worship so common among many African tribes.

The departed ancestors are the living dead and act as intermediaries between the living and the Creator.

Ugandan scholar and Christian religious philosopher, Dr. John Mbiti, has addressed the subject of traditional worship in his excellent book, *African Religions and Philosophy*.

His book was seminal work and was the first to significantly challenge Christian assumptions that traditional African religions were demonic and anti-Christian.

The Taita and other Africans who practice traditional beliefs are among those who agree with Professor Mbiti on this subject.

Besides the Taita, other people who live in the area of the Taita and Chyulu Hills are the members of the Taveta tribe. They live in the Taveta area and around Lakes Chala and Jipe.

They are not related to the Taita but they have cultural ties to both the Maasai and the Kamba who also live in the same region.

Equally important as the mountains as an integral part of culture of a number of Kenya's ethnic groups are the forests in this tropical country.

In fact, most of the forests in Kenya have some cultural significance; for example, those surrounding the sacred peak of Mount Kenya so important to the Kikuyu and related tribes, and the coastal forests surrounding the lost city-state of Gedi whose history also is of great cultural significance in terms of interaction between cultures, African and foreign, since Gedi was a product of those cultures.

There are the Aberdare mountains, simply known as the Aberdares, or Nyandarua in the Kikuyu language, which played a very important part in the history of Kenya as the sanctuary for the Mau Mau freedom fighters during the struggle for independence.

Nyandarua is, among the Kikuyu, the name for a traditional rack for drying animal skins and hides, and the spine of the Aberdare range of mountains resembles this rack.

The Kikuyu have long used the fertile slopes of the Aberdare range and it became a bone of contention between these indigenous people and the British settlers who wanted to turn Kenya into a "White Man's Country." As the first governor of Kenya, Sir Charles Eliot, a retired soldier, emphatically stated in 1905 after seizing some of the most fertile land from the Kikuyu in the central highlands:

The Protectorate is a White Man's Country. This being so, it is mere hypocrisy not to admit that white interests must be paramount and that the main object of our policy and legislation should be to found a white colony. - (Charles Eliot, *The East African Protectorate* (London: Arnold, 1905), quoted by George Padmore, *Pan-Africanism or Communism? The Coming Struggle for Africa* (London: Denis Dobson, 1956), p. 233. See also Charles Eliot quoted by Godfrey Mwakikagile, *Africa and The West* (Huntington, New York: Nova Science Publishers, Inc.,), p. 10).

The Aberdares were named after Lord Aberdare who was president of the Royal Geographic Society.

The town of Nyeri, located east of the Aberdare mountains, was the centre of the "Happy Valley" settlers during colonial times. It was a group of British aristocrats and adventurers who became notorious for their decadent lifestyles and exploits in the 1930's and 1940's. Even today, the town brings back memories of life in the olden days.

It still has the atmosphere of a sleepy English village, an impression bolstered by the cool air and morning mists which reminded the settlers of life in Britain. It was very much a cultural centre for the British during colonial times.

Just outside of the town is the Outspan Hotel, a monument to a bygone era: how life was for the white settlers in colonial times. The hotel also is the base for visitors to Treetops, another monument to the past.

The Treetops is a very important part of British history. It was here, at the Treetops, where Queen Elizabeth II was staying the night of February 6th 1952 when her father King George VI died and she had to fly back to England immediately for the funeral and as the new monarch. She was proclaimed queen the next day. It was at this forest lodge, which is surrounded by herds of buffalo and elephant, where Elizabeth officially marked her passage from princess to queen.

It was also during the same period that Mau Mau was in full swing and the Aberdares became a very important operational base and hiding place for the freedom fighters who played a critical role in speeding up the end of colonial rule in Kenya.

Today the Aberdares are a national park, and the surrounding slopes are farmland owned by the Kikuyu, the indigenous inhabitants of the area.

Another forest which is inextricably linked with the cultural life and identity of the people who live around it is the Kakamega Forest in western Kenya.

The people who live around this forest are Luhyas. Some live inside the forest and draw sustenance from it. The forest provides them with many things and has also played an important part in shaping the cultural life of the Luhya people in general.

They came from eastern Uganda and settled in Kenya during a period of major Bantu migration that lasted from 1570 to the mid-1600s.

A number of factors contributed this migration: tribal conflicts, lack of land due to high population density in their original home in eastern Uganda, and sleeping sickness.

When they arrived in the area which later became a part of a country called Kenya, they found it to be very fertile. And it came to be known as *Buluhya*, as it still is today, meaning the land or homeland of the Luhya.

Given the fertile land and abundant rainfall, together

with their skills as farmers, their new homeland was ideal for population growth and the establishment of a well-structured society. Their population grew, as did their influence in the region among other tribes, and they became some of the most successful people in Kenya.

And they are some of the most tradition-bound people in Kenya, as the structure of their society clearly shows. They have a highly complex system of clans and sub-clans unlike many other tribes in the country.

Some studies show that they may have about 750 clans, which is a very large number.

The clan system formed the basis of the Luhya form of government which revolved around powerful clan leaders called *Omwami*. And it remains the foundation of Luhya society even today.

The large number of clans had its advantages: flexibility and diversity in the traditional way of life. The Luhya did not live under a rigid, highly centralised form of government so typical of so many countries across the continent during the post-colonial period when dictatorship became institutionalised on a continental scale, with very few exceptions such as Botswana. And it is still a continental phenomenon even today under the guise of democracy.

That was not the case in traditional African societies including the Luhya.

With such great diversity of clans in Luhya society, there was ample room for experimentation and adaptation, and for innovative ideas.

Different Luhya clans had their own way of doing things and even had their own different customs not followed by other clans. And there were other differences in culture. It was basically the same Luhya culture, but with some differences among different clans.

And that is still the case today. There are many different Luhya traditions. Yet they are united as one people and follow the same practices in many areas of life.

For example, all Luhya clans practise some form of male initiation. Yet the initiation rites vary from clan to clan, ranging from traditional circumcision to the removal of lower teeth.

There are other common rituals which bind the Luhya together as a homogeneous whole and as a single cultural entity despite variations within. The sacrifice of livestock is one of them. It is used to mark rites of passage including birth and marriage.

One of the most important Luhya practices may have been adopted from the Luo who are some of their neighbours: the ceremonial driving of cattle to funerals.

Bullfighting also is one of the most well-known Luhya customs. Besides its cultural significance, it is also a very popular sport among the Luhya.

In addition to their reputation as great farmers, the Luhya have also been long known to be excellent builders and roof thatchers. But even the building of houses was based on the clan system, as it still is in many cases especially among those who still follow the traditional way of life and observe Luhya customs.

Traditional villages, known as *Itala*, were a part of a larger association of clans called *olukongo* which still exists today among many Luhyas.

The Luhya have demonstrated their skills not only as excellent builders and farmers; they also produce excellent pottery. They are also excellent weavers.

The Luhya are also known for their spectacular traditional dances. One of the most popular dances is known as *sikuti*. It is performed by groups of paired men and women to the accompaniment of a cacophony of bells and whistles.

The Luhya live in a region surrounded by Nilotic tribes. They are therefore somewhat "isolated" as a Bantu group. But they have close relatives in the region, the Kuria, whose traditional homeland was in the southern part of Kenya near the border with Tanzania.

The Kuria are also found in Tanzania in the northern region of Mara which borders Kenya and are believed to have moved south from the foothills of Mount Elgon after the Bantu migration from Uganda which centuries before started in West Africa.

Although the Kuria migrated to Kenya from Uganda as part of the Luhya migrations, they eventually developed their own customs and established a highly ritualised community.

They were known for decorating their bodies in a very spectacular way. They were also known for their highly rhythmic music and dance. Mysticism also played a major role in their lives and they were known for their skills of prophecy and rainmaking.

Another tribe related to the Kuria, hence the Luhya as well, is the Kisii. Kisii folk-role speaks of shared ancestry not just with the Kuria and the Luhya but also with the Kikuyu, the Embu and the Meru.

And like the Luhya and the Kuria, the Kisii also most likely migrated to Kenya from Uganda, settling near Lake Victoria. But the coming of the Luo in the 1700s, and later aggressive raids by the Kipsigis and the Maasai forced them to move and resettle in the highlands which are still considered to be their homeland today.

Despite the raids by the Kipsigis and the Maasai, they were not isolated and got along with the Luo who traded with them. They sold their agricultural products to the Luo and are still some of the best farmers in Kenya.

To the east in the forests of Mount Kenya emerged another culture. The forests of this majestic mountain are also the lands of the Embu and the Chuka.

The Embu are closely related to the Kikuyu and their society is organised on the basis of a close-knit clan system. Their traditional clan system is based on the extended family and all Embu clans belong to one of these groups: *Irumbi* and *Thagana*.

They are great farmers and have taken great advantage

124

of the excellent climate and fertility of the soil to grow a variety of crops and establish a strong, well-structured society in area.

Th Chuka seem to be closely related to the Embu but they are considered to be a part of the Meru. And they are all related. The Embu and the Meru are relatives as much as they are relatives of the Kikuyu, also called Gikuyu, and are - together with the Kamba (also known as Akamba) - collectively known as *Gema*, an acronym for Gikuyu, Embu, Meru, and Akamba.

The closest relatives of the Embu are the Mbeere who are also excellent farmers and beekeepers. They are also known for collecting wild honey.

Although fertile and forested regions of Kenya have helped to produce and sustain vibrant cultures and strong communities, arid lands have also made their own unique contribution to this development but mainly because of the people who settled there and the different ways they used to cope with and adapt to the harsh environment.

These are mostly the desert regions of northern Kenya including the former Northern Frontier District which is now the North Eastern Province.

Northern Kenya is the cradle of nomadic cultures in the country. And they are mostly Nilotic or Cushitic, contrasted with Bantu cultures in other parts of Kenya and whose people are mostly agriculturalists.

In fact, the remoteness of the region as well as its harsh climate and hostile environment make it one of the world's last frontiers.

It can even be described as an anthropological museum whose cultures and inhabitants together with their beasts of burden range from trips across this arid land by camel caravans of the Rendille tribe to the pride and fighting spirit of the Samburu warriors, their dances and marriage ceremonies.

The Samburu are not well-known like their relatives in the south, the Maasai, but they have a common language and share a complex culture.

An important cultural aspect of where they live – arid or not – is that their culture binds them to these ancestral lands, and the geography or the region itself has reinforced and contributed to the growth of their nomadic culture of which they are very proud and defensive.

Traditionally, Samburu communities were established in areas which provided them with an excellent view of the landscape. This appreciation of nature's beauty and the wilderness is clearly reflected in their own physical appearance which they pay great attention to. They decorate themselves and make sure they look attractive and unique as Samburu.

Even the name Samburu itself is an embodiment of beauty. It means "butterflies"and was given to them by members of another tribe or other tribes, it is said, in acknowledgement of their beauty and the time they take to make themselves look good and attractive.

Before then, they called themselves Loikop, and still do, although the term "Samburu" has gained wider currency.

Rites of passage, or initiation, and warrior culture constitute the backbone of Samburu society. They are some of the most important aspects of their life as a people which distinguish them from other tribes and give meaning to their temporal existence and even the spiritual dimension of their very being.

Their society is based on age groups defined by a custom called *Olpiroi*, which means "fire-stick."

The "fire-stick" is handed down, from one age-set to the next, as one generation of *morani* (warriors) becomes responsible for the moral and cultural education of the next. This practice is the foundation not only of the age-hierarchy among the Samburu but also of respect for customs and traditions which hold the community together with its own identity.

Although they differ in some ways in terms of how

they live and how they decorate and even see themselves, the Samburu share some customs with their relatives, the Maasai. For example, the blessing of cattle, preparation for war, and victory in a hunt, all of which are celebrated by the Maasai, are also celebrated by the Samburu. And when Samburu warriors dance, they leap high just like the Maasai do, encouraged by the cries of other warriors.

Other similarities between the Samburu and the Maasai include the design and style of the beads they were. The beading is done by women but it is worn by both men and women. But Samburu women don't wear the large flat necklaces Maasai women do. Instead, they wear single loop bead necklaces given to them by their admirers, mostly the *morani*. They are given frequently and soon together form a thick collar.

The Samburu believe that when a girl reaches the age of 15 or 16, she should have enough loops of beads around her neck to support her chin. When she achieves that, she's ripe or ready for marriage.

The nomadic life style of the Samburu is one of the most distinctive features of their culture. And they ride camels well-suited to the arid region of northern Kenya. They travel long distances in search of pasture and water for their cows, sheep, and goats.

Traditionally, they did not have camels. They acquired them in recent years and got the idea of having these animals probably from the Rendille and the Turkana with whom they have a close relationship and who also live in northern Kenya.

They are so proud of their nomadic life and of being pastoralists that they view farming and any other kind of economic activity that requires settled living as something that is beneath them.

And you really don't find farmers in northern Kenya; not the kind you see, for example, in the central highlands or in western Kenya. The north is nomadic country.

Also living in the northern part of Kenya are the

Borana, or Boran, who originally came from Ethiopia. In fact, there is still a tribe in Ethiopia with the same name. And Marsabit, located in the central part of northern Kenya, lies at the heart of the ancestral homelands of these people who are very proud of their culture and life style.

Linguistically, the Borana are related to the Galla who include the Oromo. But there is a fundamental difference between the two. The Borana are nomadic; the Galla, agricultural. And the name Borana means "free," in reference to their nomadic life style.

The Borana migrated from Ethiopia to Kenya around 1720 and are therefore relatively new to the region. But during the years they have been there, they have roamed the entire vast expanse in keeping with their nomadic life style.

However, something happened in the 1960s which had a profound impact on their lives. It was a period of major cultural change caused by conflict.

During that period, they had many conflicts with Somali cattle bandits who also roamed the region and the Borana were forced to give up their cattle herds and turn – almost exclusively – to camel husbandry. It was a major and painful change since cattle ownership was, and still is, seen as a symbol of status and a sign of great wealth among most nomads in northern Kenya.

The shift had an even bigger impact on the Borana because cattle ownership was very much an integral part of their cultural identity. This was compounded by the negative attitude the Galla, their relatives, had towards camel ownership.

They considered camels to be lowly and inferior creatures, far beneath cows, and anyone who owned them was equally inferior. This was devastating to the Borana. They went through a fundamental cultural change they never anticipated – until the Somali bandits struck. The change was, in a way, a culture shock.

The Borana society is basically a structure whose

building blocks are family-based clans. Thus, a clan is a collection of related families. The underlying cultural principle of the society is *gada*, an age-set system.

The *gada* principle governs the way a man lives almost his entire life. The first 40 years of a male Borana is divided into five eight-year periods.

There are specific beliefs which clearly show what a man may or may not do during each eight-year period, and strict observance of these believes is expected of every man in the Borana society. For example, they show in which eight-year period a man should marry, settle, and have children.

Many Boranas have been converted to Islam and, to a smaller degree, to Christianity. But there are those who still follow traditional religious beliefs. The beliefs are based on reverence for both the supernatural and the natural. Water is seen as a blessing from the heavens, and grass (especially for their livestock, which are camels nowadays) from the earth.

Maintenance of peace within the Borana community is a fundamental principle. The principle is known as *Nagya Borana*, which basically means "Peace of the Boran," and it is the basis of Boran culture. The Boran people believe that all members of the society must at all times be guided by this principle, seek and maintain peace that unites their entire community.

Even when they have conflicts with other tribes, the Boran (or Borana) are always taught to remember that they must maintain peace among themselves. Nothing from outside should be allowed to divide them or cause conflict within the community.

The Boran are closely related to the Gabbra who are also found in many parts of northern Kenya. Like the Boran, they also own camels.

Another tribe of camel owners in this region is the Rendille. But the Rendille are not related to the Boran or the Gabbra. They are, instead, closely related to the

Somali who mostly live in northeastern Kenya but from whom they are physically separated by the lands owned by Gabbra-speaking communities.

The Rendille have a reputation as excellent camel herders and handlers and they live as typical nomads, very proud of their nomadic way of life, and very defensive of their life style. They have designed special saddles which enable their camels to carry the entire possessions of a household when families move form one place to another; an achievement - among many others - that enhances their nomadic culture.

An interesting development has taken place between the Rendille and the Samburu through the years. Although the two tribes are not linguistically and genetically related, they have forged strong links between them leading to a strong relationship that has resulted in intermarriage.

One of the most important results of this bond between the two groups has been the evolution of a hybrid culture, in some cases, that has taken place through the years. The culture is neither typical Rendille nor typical Samburu; nor is it entirely alien. But it is unique in its own way as a product of the two.

However, distinct Samburu and Rendille cultures still exist despite the fusion of the two which has taken place in a number of cases. The hybrid culture is not typical of either one.

The focal point of this geographic "wasteland" is Marsabit, a small town whose lush and fertile oasis draws many people of different cultures from all parts of the arid region of northern Kenya.

The intermingling of these people has also led to an intermingling of cultures, making Marsabit some sort of cultural capital or the cosmopolitan centre of northern Kenya. The streets of this small town are a display of different ethnic identities.

There are the Boran, the Rendille, the Samburu, the Gabbra, the Somali, and even the Ethiopians in this region bordering Ethiopia. Add to the mix, tourists from different parts of the world, and even Kenyans of other tribes from the south who now and then visit the north. It is a dazzling array of cultures.

Just as the deserts, mountains and forests have played a critical role in shaping the cultures of the people who live in and around those areas, so has the wilderness.

Human culture has evolved and emerged in the wilderness in many parts of the world throughout man's history, and Kenya is no exception.

For many Kenyan indigenous tribes, life is inextricably linked with nature, in its natural state, and with forces that are sometimes beyond man's control; for example, thunder and lightning, floods, drought and famine, and much more. They all shape man's destiny, hence culture, as they have in Kenya.

They have developed a unique balance between human culture and the wilderness. They live in cooperation with, not in confrontation with, nature and, have in a way, tamed nature. They are not trying to conquer nature.

Among the best examples of those people are the Maasai. And Amboseli, a major tourist attraction, is an integral part of Maasai culture and way of life. It is located in an area that is considered to be, and which is indeed, their homeland. It has therefore been very much shaped by them as it has, in a way, shaped them.

Amboseli is part of Maasailand in the southern part of Kenya close to the border with Tanzania. And for as long as they have lived here, the Maasai have traversed the vast expanse of territory with their herds in search of water and pasture.

The border between the two countries, a colonial creation, means nothing to them. They were there before Europeans came and partitioned Africa and, in their way of life, they don't recognise the boundary which separates the two countries. They accept the fact that the border separates Kenya and Tanzania but they know, and don't accept, that it separates them.

Many of the lodges and camps in Amboseli which are used by tourists and other visitors are an integral part of the Maasai. They work closely with the Maasai communities which surround this place. And many tourists visit Maasai villages, with the help of Maasai tour guides, and spend time with the Maasai.

Amboseli National Park is not only surrounded by many Maasai villages; there is also a small Maasai town, Oloitoktok, which provides visitors with a majestic view of Mount Kilimanjaro in neighbouring Tanzania. The town has large markets filled with the Maasai from surrounding areas and anyone visiting this place gets the chance to know not only about the Maasai as a people but also about their culture.

On the other side of the country is one of the places called Laikipia which is in a region considered to be the gateway to Kenya's wild northern frontier. It is sparsely populated but much of Laikipia is covered by large privately-owned ranches.

This is Samburu country. It is also the land of the Kalenjin, a collection of related tribes, one of the biggest being the Pokot whose members are one of the tribes which live in this area that includes the Laikipia National Reserve.

The Pokot have an interesting culture just like the rest of the Kenyan tribes do, although each in its unique way. And that's what makes it so interesting in each case.

Although they are one tribe, the Pokot are divided into two distinct groups, something which gives them a unique identity among Kenyan tribes and even within the Kalenjin community. One is composed of the people of the cattle, called *Pi pa Tix*. It is a group of cattle herders. The other one, known as *Pi pa Pax*, is made of the people of the maize. It is a group of farmers.

No other Kenyan tribe is divided this way, a cultural attribute which has made the Pokot a subject of enduring fascination among many people including anthropologists and other researchers. The lifestyles of the two groups are also different in many fundamental respects. Even the houses they build for themselves are designed differently, emphasising the difference between them. Yet they are united as one people.

And despite the division between the two groups, Pokot culture is essentially a nomadic culture centred on cattle. Even the people of the maize, the farmers among the Pokot, own cows.

Another cultural attribute which makes the Pokot stand out has to do with their customs and traditions. The customs and traditions and even physical adornments of the Pokot are more closely linked to the Karamajong of Uganda than they are to the customs and traditions and bodily decorations of the other Kalenjin people.

Ownership of cows has always been very important to the Pokot, and they see bulls as very special to them. The most important bulls are called *kmar*. It is an ox with distinctive horns. One is curved forward, and the other one, backwards.

They hold them in reverence and are a very important part of their religious beliefs. Throughout their history, the Pokot have had a very close relationship with these bulls which borders on mystical worship.

The Pokot have been culturally influenced by the Teso-Karamajong but this cultural influence is stronger among the Pokot who belong to the group of the people of the cattle, what the Pokot call *Pi pa Tix*.

The Teso-Karamajong influence over the Pokot extends into the realm of initiation. Like many Kenyan tribes, the people of the maize have adopted initiation rituals based on rites of circumcision. But the people of the cattle do not circumcise just like the Teso-Karamajong don't. Like the Teso-Karamajong, they consider the practice to be barbaric.

While the people of the cattle disapproved of

circumcision as an initiation rite, they developed their own rite of initiation called *sapana*. Initiation by this ritual meant entry into one of two social categories in the Potok community. One was *tukoi* (meaning zebra), so called because of the distinctive pattern of their brass jewellery. The other one was called *nyimur* , which means stone, and was named that way in reference to their dark copper jewellery.

Competition for land due to increased population has forced many Pokots to turn to agriculture. This has been a fundamental change in the lives of many members of this community, a departure from their traditional way of life as pastoralists and nomads.

But, in spite of the changes which have taken place in the Pokot society in modern times, one thing remains unchanged: their traditions and customs, and their traditional attire as well as their distinctive folk music remain fully rooted in the influences of western Kenya and eastern Uganda.

Laikipia is home to several community ranches owned and managed by local communities to protect wildlife, communal lands and areas for pasture in this cattle-centred society. The communities have combined small-scale farms and grazing land to establish group ranches which are a big attraction to tourists.

The tourist trade has proved to be far more profitable than agriculture or animal husbandry, allowing local communities to use their traditional lands in a very productive way. The ranches have bolstered a sense of local identity and strengthened community ties. And they provide a perfect setting for outsiders to learn about local cultures by staying on the ranches with the members of those communities. The ranches have guest houses, home stays and private camps.

On these ranches, members of the local communities are not only conserving wildlife; they are preserving their traditional way of life.

It is a functional relationship between nature - the wilderness and the wildlife - and man, and the Pokot as well as other tribes of the Kalenjin community have been able to preserve their cultures in this region with little disturbance in their traditional way of life.

Another wilderness area that is an integral part of the traditional way of life of the people who live around there is Maasai Mara which, like Amboseli, is part of Maasailand.

The Maasai once roamed a vast expanse of what is Kenya today, especially from the central part of the country all the way to the southern part. Today, they live mostly in southwestern Kenya.

They have ancestral ties to the Samburu and the Njemps with whom they share a language, Maa, and from which the name Maasai comes. They lead an entirely nomadic life style as cattle herders.

It is only in recent times that some of them have become farmers and have engaged in other economic activities besides owning cows around which revolves virtually everything else in the Maasai traditional way of life.

In fact, cows are central to their religious beliefs. They believe that God, whom they call *Enkai*, gave them cows as a gift. To them cows are sacred. Grass also is sacred and is considered to be a blessing.

Maasai mythology tells of a time when the earth and the sky were joined together. Then there came a time when the two were suddenly separated. But there was something that still connected them: fig trees.

The trees were left to serve as a bridge between the earth and the sky. It was these trees, the Maassi believe, which God used to send cows down from heaven to the Maasai as a gift to them.

Even today, the Maasai have great respect for fig trees, as they do for grass. Whenever they pass a fig tree, it is customary for the Maasai – at least more often than not –

to push handfuls of grass between the roots of the tree as homage.

The Maasai also consider wildlife to be sacred, just like the cows and the grass. The wildebeest, especially, have a special place in the hearts of the Maasai because of the role the herds of these animals play to regenerate the grasslands.

Lions, although they attack cattle, also play an important role in Maasai culture. They are traditionally respected but those which attack cows are hunted and killed.

Hunting lions also is a ceremonial event in Maasai culture, giving young Maasai men, known as *morani*, a chance to prove their manhood and show courage. After killing a lion, victorious hunters return to their village and perform a traditional dance called *engilakinoto*.

The dance is not only a climax of manhood, showing that the young men have proved to be manly and courageous by killing this dangerous animal; it has great cultural significance as a demonstration of Maasai commitment to the preservation of their culture which holds them together as a people with their own distinct identity.

The Maasai also dance to bless their cattle and when they prepare for war.

They also have a highly complex system of initiation and age-sets. The first step in initiation for boys within the same age-group is circumcision. Next is a period of recovery, or convalescence, during which boys wear black and cover their faces with white powder.

After they do all that, the young men are considered to be junior *morani*. The *morani*, or Wamorani as they are called in Kiswahili, grow their hair into long braids which they usually decorate with red ochre.

They also use red ochre to slather their upper bodies. This is a very important colour to the Maasai. It is considered to be sacred and is their favourite with great cultural and religious significance.

The beading the Maasai wear also has great cultural and religious significance. They use red, blue and green beads when they do bead-work. This is done by women but won by both. The red symbolises the Maasai as a people. Blue beads are considered to be divinely, reflecting the colour of the sky hence symbolising heaven. And green is the colour of God's greatest blessing, fresh grass after rainfall, which nourishes and sustains their cattle.

Unmarried women wear necklaces made of rows of beads when dancing. The necklaces look like large flat discs and the women use the movement of the discs when dancing to emphasise their lithe movements. One of the most common dances for women is *olamal* which is used to attract blessings from community leaders.

Mothers also play an important part in the initiation of their sons into manhood, even if their role is more symbolic than functional.

When a son gets ready to be initiated, he is given pedants by his mother to wear throughout the initiation process. The pedants are known as *surutia* and they are later given back to the mother for her to wear as a sign of her son's status and pride for her child. She wears them for the rest of her life and will remove them only if her son dies.

When the young men become *morani*, they usually start to travel throughout Maasailand, visiting various communities along the way. It is part of the Maasai culture and a cultural obligation for them to do so.

And when they return to their homes and villages, a ceremony is held for them. It is called *eunoto* and their heads are shaved by their mothers. This symbolises a major transition, passage from junior *morani* to senior *morani*. Once they go through this, they are considered to be mature enough to marry.

As in most, if not in all, African societies, elders are

highly respected in the Maasai society and are regarded as a repository of knowledge and wisdom and custodians of Maasai culture. They carry a large walking stick or a *rungu* to symbolise their high status in society. Judgement on critical matters is deferred to them.

The most respected, and most revered, of all the Maasai elders are called *laiboni*. They are traditional prophets, seers and healers. The *laiboni* have always played a paramount role in Maasai society.

In fact, the Maasai way of life is a rite of passage, from birth to death, marked by ceremonies and celebrations and strict observance of Maasai customs and traditions. Some of these ceremonies include the use of milk which is considered to be sacred, like the cows themselves. It is used to bestow blessings. If milk is not available, white dust is used instead.

Many Maasai ceremonies involve the ritual slaughter of cows or goats, with meat being distributed among community members according to rank in society. Maasai villages are called *manyata*.

The Maasai are a very independent people. Ritual and tradition is an integral part of their everyday lives. They live close to nature and in harmony with nature. They see themselves as part of the land, and land as part of them, forming an organic whole with a spiritual dimension.

They rarely hunt. Living in harmony with wildlife is part of their beliefs. Lions and wildebeest play an important role in their cultural beliefs as much as their own cows do.

They are an integral part of each other in a harmonious universe the Maasai have constructed for themselves and for the wildlife, based on their beliefs, and in which cooperation rather than confrontation prevails.

Strict adherence to their traditions, customs and beliefs has enabled the Maasai to maintain their identity through generations in a way many African tribes have not been able to. Their culture remains intact and is virtually unassailable.

Another tribe whose cultural fabric is interwoven with the natural environment is the Meru.

Together with the Kikuyu (or Gikuyu) and the Embu, they constitute a collective identity which is one of the most interesting cultural phenomena in Kenya.

In fact, the Meru tribe itself is a collective entity comprising several groups whose members share a common identity. These groups are the Igembe, the Chuka, the Igoji, the Imenti, the Muitini, the Muthambi, Mwimbi, and the Tigania.

The name "Meru" comes from the Maasai language and it has to do with forests. The Maasai called the forests of Imenti and Tigania, "Mieru,"meaning "a quiet place." The term can also be used in the Maasai language to describe a people who can not understand *Maa*, which is the name of the Maasai language.

And the home district of the Meru is named after the Meru tribe and is called Meru District.

The territory occupied by the Meru covers a large area and forms a kind of cultural bridge between the coastal region and Mount Kenya. And the Meru trace their origin to an area in the northern part of the coastal region of Kenya.

All the groups which constitute the Meru tribe share a common legend about their origins, with the exception of one group, the Chuka.

They say they followed the Tana River inland and spread widely across the northeast, reaching the forests of Mount Kenya. When they arrived in this area, they began to adopt cultural practices from inland nomadic cultures, including the Maasai, but retained their original clan system. The Meru are divided into three clans: Njiru, Ntune, and Njaru.

Among the cultural practices they adopted from the inland nomadic tribes were warrior culture from the Maasai; making spears like the Boran do; and excluding fish from their diet, which was quite a change for a people who said they originally came from the coast where eating fish was and still is so common.

The Chuka are the furthest removed from the coastal origin of the Meru and many researchers now believe that they are probably not related to the rest of the Meru but are more closely related to the Embu. The history of the Chuka is one of hunt gatherers who eventually became farmers, clearly showing that they were not a coastal people where there was hardly any hunting done.

In fact, the Chuka share many customs with the Embu, including the way they sing and dance. The Chuka music and dance has a unique style of drumming using drums of the Kamba tribe.

A different tribe living in the area of what is now Meru National Park is the Thakara.

The origins of the Thakara are also uncertain but they lived in isolation in the the Tana Valley which enabled them to develop a culture that was not influenced by other tribes.

Traditionally, the Thakara were widely known and highly respected as makers of weapons and practitioners of traditional medicine. They were also well-known for their ornate clothing including distinctive leather skirts and long aprons decorated with cowrie shells for women; and animal skin cloaks and feathered headdresses for men.

People who go to Meru are also able to learn about Meru culture not only from the people themselves but also from the museum in Meru town. The museum has an assortment of displays on Meru culture.

The area of Meru was also the scene of one of the best known stories about nature. It was in Meru where George and Joy Adamson released a captive lioness into the wild in the 1950's. The event became the subject of a bestselling book, *Born Free*. And a film based on the story won an Academy Award.

The significance of this event was two-fold. It showed

that man can live in harmony with nature, including wild animals. The lioness returned a number of times to visit the Adamsons at their camp before going back to the wild where she had adapted to the environment and the wildlife with other lions She even took her cubs with her to visit them.

The event was also a powerful appeal for conservation of wildlife and its habitat and made the Adamsons icons of the conservation movement worldwide.

What is also important to remember is that the people of many different tribes in Kenya, and in other parts of Africa, have great respect for the wild animals which live in the same areas they do. It has to do with respect for nature, and their belief that they can co-exist in harmony as long as the people have their own area, and animals also have their own space.

One of the most well-known wilderness areas in Kenya is Tsavo. It is in the region which is the home of the Kamba tribe.

The Kamba have a well-developed oral history about their origin. They say they came from what later became the country of Tanganyika, now Tanzania. But their history also has two versions. One says they came from what is now western Tanzania; another says they came from the plains around Mount Kilimanjaro.

There is, however, some agreement on how they lived before they migrated to what is Kenya today. They lived as semi-nomads, herding, hunting, and sometimes farming.

The arrival of the Iloikop Maasai in the 16th century forced them to leave northeastern Tanganyika (Tanzania), driving them northwards. They crossed the rocky Chyulu hills and settled at Mbooni, in the highlands that would take their name and become known as Ukambani.

The Kamba dispersed and roamed widely over the plains of Tsavo, establishing many small settlements. They were excellent hunters and trappers, highly regarded for their archery skills, skills which served them well when they joined the colonial army and the police in highly disproportionate numbers. They were well-suited for the job because of their "natural" ability as hunters.

They were also great elephant hunters and from the 18th century became involved in the ivory trade, supplying Swahili merchants on the coast. These commercial ties enable the Kamba to get goods they never had before, including copper wire and bright blue calico which became part of their already ornate tribal regalia and ornamentation.

The Kamba are still known for their wood carving skills – like the Makonde are in Tanzania and Mozambique – and are considered to be the best carvers in Kenya.

The Kamba were also well-known for their gifts of prophecy. During the latter part of the 19th century, Kamba seers predicted a time of great and turbulent change ahead which would have tremendous impact on the African way of life.

The Kikuyu also had a prophecy: "There shall come a people with clothes like butterflies." Kenyan writer Ngugi wa Thiong'o - who is a Kikuyu himself - used the prophecy as the beginning of his novel, *The River Between.*

And both, the Kamba and the Kikuyu seers, were vindicated by history. Shortly thereafter, or after only a few years, the white man arrived. And, as the saying goes, the rest is history.

One of the most dramatic events which had to do with the coming of the white man was the construction - by the British - of what came to be known as the Uganda Railway from Mombasa on the Kenyan coast to the shores of Lake Victoria in western Kenya. And one of the main objectives in building this railway was to consolidate white domination over the Kenya.

Africans called the railway, the Iron Snake, and saw it

not only as something strange and alien but also as malevolent. Again, they were vindicated by history. The railway played a critical role in establishing and consolidating colonial rule to the detriment of the indigenous people. Among the victims were, of course, the Kamba.

And after the British failed to recruit enough local labour to build the railway, they turned to their colony of India where they recruited thousands of Gujarati and brought them to Kenya.

The arrival of the Indians also had a major impact on the country. It opened the way for the settlement of tens of thousands of Indians in this East African country, forever changing the cultural landscape of Kenya.

It was also in Kamba country where one of the most blood-curdling stories about life in the wilderness was recorded.

When the railway from Mombasa reached the Tsavo River in 1899, the British were faced with a major task of building a major bridge across this river. They built a camp, occupied mostly by the Indian railroad workers. Then terror began.

The workers were repeatedly attacked and dragged out of their tents at night by lions. Then the lions became even bolder and attacked in broad daylight.

The culprits were two male lions. They eluded capture with such ease as if they had supernatural intelligence. They were able to avoid hunting parties, ambush or any trap, and even escaped from traps.

The indigenous people, including the Kamba who lived in the area, had a different interpretation of all this. They believed that the lions were spirits and ghosts who had been transformed into physical entities to drive the British away from Kenya. And it made a lot of sense to them. No one had invited the British to Kenya, let alone asked them to build the railway across the country and colonise the people.

The lions killed 124 people in one year. All were railroad workers, and most were Indians. The construction of the bridge was stopped, and the workers were terrified to continue working.

Finally, after persevering for a long time, Colonel James Patterson, who was one of the British engineers working on the railway, tracked down the two lions and shot them dead. And a legend was born.

He was lionised in Kenya and in Britain, and in other countries, as the man who brought down the beasts and later wrote a bestselling book, *The Maneaters of Tsavo*. One hundred years later, Hollywood turned the story into a sensational film, but with embellishments, to entertain, and not accurately reflecting the events that took place in that part of Kamba country in Kenya.

What happened at Tsavo also became part of the history of Kambaland or Ukambani. Patterson's book was also translated into Kiswahili and entitled, *Simba wa Tsavo*, which means "Lions of Tsavo."

The two lions became a permanent feature of the Chicago Field Museum in Chicago, the United States, where they still are today.

Besides mountains, deserts, forests, and the wilderness, lakes have also been centres of culture and civilisation throughout man's history, only in varying degrees, depending on the people and the environment in different parts of the world. And Kenya is no exception.

Each of Kenya's lakes is unique, and each has its own unique culture and local history.

One of those lakes is Lake Baringo, the traditional home of the Njemps people.

The Njemps are linguistically related to both the Maasai and the Samburu. It is also possible they are genetically related to one or both of them.

They have many cultural ties to both the Maasai and the Samburu. And it is possible that they are descended from a Samburu clan known as the Il-Doigo or Maasai

144

clan driven out of the Laikipia area by inter-clan warfare. Whatever the case, they have indissoluble ties to both.

Regardless of where they came from, it is an established fact that they moved into an area known as Njemps south and southwest of Lake Baringo and adopted that name.

Although they kept many of the customs of the Maasai and the Samburu, they developed a very different lifestyle in their new home region. They abandoned the nomadic way of life and became farmers. And although the soil around Lake Baringo is not fertile, they developed a highly sophisticated system of irrigation and grew crops on the shores of the lake.

Throughout the 19th century, they sold their agricultural products to passing caravans of explorers and traders, leading them to develop even better agricultural skills because of their success in this business. This form of trade was completely alien to their Maasai and Samburu relatives, clearly showing that after they left one of these tribes, they went on to forge a totally new identity in terms of lifestyle.

They went even further and became fishermen as well. This was a radical departure from tradition and it set them apart from their relatives, the Maasai and the Samburu, in a way that seemed incomprehensible. To a Maasai or a Samburu, eating fish is taboo. Even today, most Maasai and Samburu won't even touch, let alone eat, fish. And they react with revulsion to any suggestion or idea that eating fish is good for your health.

When they settled around lake Baringo, the Njemps took advantage of the abundance of fish in the lake. The fish became not only a major part of their diet but also a major source of income.

They use canoes built from a local reed and use them for fishing. The boats look extremely unstable and flimsy but they are strong enough to transport heavy loads and live goats and sheep across the lake.

The Njemps often fish on the shore using nets and lines and hardly show any fear of the many crocodiles found in the lake. People are attacked by crocodiles now and then but the Njempas have adapted to the environment and know how to survive. The lake also has many hippos which can be dangerous to human beings.

But there is no challenge that the Njemps have not been able to overcome in this area. Their distinctive lifestyle is also well-suited to the environment.

In fact, the Njemps are the only pastoral, cattle-herding tribe who also fish.

Another lake, Lake Turkana which was known as Lake Rudolph until the 1970's, is in an area inhabited by some of the most conservative tribes in Africa in terms of lifestyle. They are the Turkana after whom the lake is named.

In fact, the sheer remoteness of this inland lake has insulated from foreign influence the people who live around it. Their cultures have remained virtually intact, uncontaminated, unlike those of other people in other parts of Kenya.

The roots of the Turkana lie not in Kenya but in southern Sudan and in Uganda among the Karamajong. They migrated to the lake area about 250 years ago.

It is an inhospitable area, with baking fields of lava surrounding crocodile infested waters. It's hot, it's dry, it's stifling.

But the Turkana are great survivors, with great endurance, known throughout Kenya for their survival skills, physical strength and aggressive opportunism. Throughout Kenya, they are regarded as the toughest and most aggressive people on earth.

They have spread throughout this part of northern Kenya of arid country and have survived and thrived under the most difficult conditions. They are survivors.

They are mainly cattle herders. But they are also hunters and gatherers in this harsh environment and have been compelled to diversify their economic activities just to survive. Fish, crocodiles and other wildlife are part of their traditional diet.

Their traditional society is based on the clan system which is anchored in the formation of cattle raiding parties. Cattle raiding is central to their culture.

And in spite of the harsh environment in which they live, making life difficult, the Turkana still have time for beauty. They have a highly developed sense of the aesthetic and it is an integral part of their culture. They produce a great deal of jewellery and articles of physical adornment.

Turkana men have highly developed skills in combat and have for long made a wide range of weapons in a very innovative way.

The Turkana in general are also excellent craftsmen, skilled in metalwork, leather-making, beading and carving of wood, stone, and other material.

Other people who live with the Turkana in the same region are the Samburu, the Rendille and the Gabbra.

On the southern shores of Lake Turkana are the El Molo, Kenya's smallest tribe. It is a remarkable contrast. Members of the smallest tribe in Kenya live on the shores of the largest permanent desert lake in the world. It is more than 250 kilometres long, longer than the entire coast of Kenya, and has the world's single largest crocodile population.

The El Molo are also some of Kenya's last remaining true hunter gatherers. They survive almost entirely on fishing, using nets made from a local palm fibre, and simple log canoes. They are also know for their great skills in weaving baskets and fishing nets.

They have lost some of their culture because of increasing intermarriage with the Turkana and the Samburu, bigger tribes which have gradually absorbed them. They have also adopted the languages of these two tribes.

Unfortunately, this intermarriage and linguistic and cultural absorption, and assimilation, will eventually lead to the extinction of an indigenous group of people and one of the last true hunter-gatherer communities in the entire world. It may, indeed, be a form of genocide for them.

One of the largest lakes in the world has also been one of the most important sources of sustenance for a large number of cultural communities who live around it.

One of those groups is the Luo who live on the shores of Lake Victoria which is also the second-largest freshwater lake in the world after Lake Superior in North America. They also live in the rest of Nyanza Province bordering the lake.

They are a resourceful people, their resourcefulness and vitality partly fuelled by the abundance of Lake Victoria, and by their spirit of adventure and survival which animated them when they trekked south from Sudan in search of a better life; a quest that finally took them to their present home in western Kenya close to Lake Victoria whose African name is Nyanza.

They originally came from a region known as Bahr el Ghazal in southern Sudan, a region through which River Nile flows north from Lake Victoria.

So, in a way, even before they migrated to what is Kenya today, they have had some kind of ties to Lake Victoria because of River Nile whose waters provided sustenance to their original home region in Sudan long before they migrated south, first settling in what later became the country of Uganda.

The migration from Uganda, going east to Kenya, began in the 16th century and involved many small groups which eventually settled on the eastern shores of Lake Victoria. A hybrid culture evolved among these various disparate peoples until a truly unique and independent society emerged by the late 19th century.

Many of the different tribal groups which constituted this wave of migration were cattle herders and nomads.

But their lifestyles underwent fundamental change because of changed circumstances.

The abundant water supplies from Lake Victoria, combined with physical restrictions of tribal lands - which had already been taken by other tribes - and then colonial boundaries which led to the establishment of Kenya and Uganda, compelled them to shift towards farming and fishing.

They could no longer move freely and occupy any land they wanted to occupy. The land had either already been taken or was restricted by tribal boundaries and colonial demarcations.

Although the Luo abandoned the nomadic way of life when they settled in Kenya, cattle ownership still played a central role in their culture. In many Luo traditions and customs, bulls occupied a special place; and so did the size of a man's herd. The more cows you had, the richer and more powerful and influential you were. And that is still the case today as much as it is in many other African traditional societies in which people own cows.

In Luo culture, cattle provided more than just meat and milk. After slaughter, every part of the cow was used, from leather to hoofs – leather was used as a sleeping mat , and hoofs as containers for herbal medicine; and from head to tail – the hair of the tail was used to make traps for birds.

Lake Victoria has also played an important religious role in Luo culture because it is believed to have divine powers, determining the fate of the Luo nation.

In their traditional religion, the Luo had two deities: a supreme god called Nyasai, and Chieng, the sun. Ancestors and ancestral spirits played a critical role in their religious beliefs, providing a guiding hand to the living in their journey through life.

And they still do today, although not as much as before because of the influence of Christianity and Western civilisation both of which have had a profound impact on the traditional way of life among many Luos, especially those who have had some education.

Rites for death and funerals are also central to Luo culture. Traditional funerals include a protracted period of mourning, the shaving of heads of male relatives of the departed, and the running of herds of cattle through the family compound.

Although the Luo are divided into 40 clans, they are bound together as one people by a cohesive network of clans which constitutes a solid foundation for the tribal community.

And from the time they abandoned their pastoral way of life, ownership of land has played a central role in Luo life and culture. The Luo take land ownership very seriously, not only as a means of survival but as a basis for their very existence as a collective entity.

Traditionally, land was divided on the basis of clans. And each clan was ruled by a prominent figure who gained prominence – and was chosen – because he had a lot of wealth, wives and children.

Clan leaders were essentially landlords called *ruoth* and were protected by warriors and spiritual leaders. Warriors were known as *thuondi*, and spiritual leaders were called *jabilo*.

Luo warriors had a reputation as great fighters and hunters. They were also highly regard for their strength. Among the animals they hunted was the hippo, which was a major challenge given the hippo's large size, strength and aggressive nature especially when confronted.

But the Luo did not lead an entirely peaceful life. They were attacked by the Nandi, a tribe of formidable and fearless warriors, forcing them to build stone fortresses for protection.

The change in lifestyle the Luo have undergone through the centuries since they arrived in what is Kenya today has been dramatic. They not only became agriculturalists after leading a pastoral life in their original homeland in Sudan; the Luo who settled around Lake Victoria also became fishermen, in addition to being farmers and cattle owners. Many Luos depend on fishing to earn a living.

The impact of western civilisation on the Luo society has been disruptive in some ways. It remains a close-knit community but it also has lost some of its traditions through the years.

But even the adoption of Christianity has not fundamentally changed the Luo way of life in all aspects although it has among some people. The spread of Christianity among Luos has also led to the creation of small sects which combine Christian teachings with traditional beliefs, a hybrid which many Luos believe serves them well since it also enables them to preserve their traditional way of life and forms of worship while at the same time practising Christianity.

In Seme, not far from Kisumu is a massive rock called Kit Maye which has long been considered sacred by Luos. It has, in traditional beliefs, been regarded as having supernatural powers and has played a central in Luo culture through the years.

Traditionally, the rock was visited by those seeking blessings, favour or divine intervention. Animal or token sacrifices were made beneath Kit Maye, and even today some believe that visiting the site or leaving sacrifices will result in blessings and good luck.

This is one of the best examples of the power of traditional beliefs not only among the Luo but among other Africans as well.

While the interior of Kenya has cultures which are predominantly African, with many people living the traditional way of life the way their ancestors did for centuries before the coming of foreigners, many parts of the coastal region are characterised by cultures which are an eclectic mix of the traditional ways of life and foreign influences from the Arab world, Asia, and Europe.

The eclectic nature of these cultures is best exemplified by Swahili culture, a mix, blend and fusion of mostly African and Arab cultures.

The coastal region has a long history, in fact the longest among all regions of Kenya in terms of contact with foreign cultures, especially those of the Arab world and Asia, but mainly of the Arab world.

Although the Portuguese established a presence in Mombasa, they did not leave much of an impact on the coast in terms of culture and other aspects of life besides architecture at Fort Jesus.

Life in places like Lamu and Mombasa has remained basically unchanged for centuries. But it still, since the arrival of the Arabs centuries ago, has been a blend of African and Arab cultures and therefore has had a dynamic of its own through the years. It is not typical African, nor is it typical Arab but a synthesis of the two.

And it is a synthesis that gives Kenya its unique character. Cultures have merged to form new cultural identities not only in the coastal areas but in other parts of the country as well.

There are also many cultures which have remained virtually intact through the centuries and retained their true African identity, typical examples being the Turkana and the Samburu which have had very little foreign influences not only because of their remoteness but mainly because of the refusal of the people themselves to be influenced by outsiders in terms of values, traditions and customs.

Kenya may not have a lot of natural resources – gold and diamonds, and other minerals – but it is a cultural goldmine.

There is no other country in East Africa (a region composed of Kenya, Uganda and Tanzania) or in the entire region of eastern Africa (that includes the Horn of Africa) which has the kind of ethnic and cultural diversity that Kenya has, and on such a large scale.

Kenya's indigenous population is of Bantu stock as

well as Nilotic and Cushitic. It is the only country in East Africa which has a very large number of people of Cushitic origin.

Tanzania has Cushitic tribes, especially in the north-central part of the country, whose members - mainly the Iraqw - migrated from southern Ethiopia centuries ago. It also has a significant number of Somalis, and a significant number of people of Nilotic origin including the Maasai. But not as much as Kenya does.

The number of people of Nilotic and Cushitic descent in Kenya far surpasses that of Tanzanians of the same origin. Uganda has, if any in significant numbers, even fewer people of Cushitic origin, although it does have large numbers of people of Nilotic descent and more than Tanzania does.

Ethiopia, Somalia, Eritrea and Djibouti don't have any Bantu tribes. They also don't have any Nilotic groups with the possible exception of Ethiopia in the western part of the country bordering Kenya and Sudan, and may be some in western Eritrea that also borders Sudan.

It is only Kenya which has all those groups – Bantu, Nilotic and Cushitic – in large numbers as tribes and as an integral part of the total population. And they are native to Kenya although they migrated there from other parts of Africa. But as ethnic groups, they have lived in Kenya long enough to qualify as natives of the country, and legitimately claim the areas where they live as their homelands.

The cultures of all those people have made Kenya unique, not only in East Africa but in the entire region of eastern Africa.

Chapter Seven:

Ethnic Conflicts in Kenya: A Nation Divided

ALTHOUGH Kenya has been spared the agony Rwanda went through during the 1994 genocide which amounted to ethnic cleansing, and even what neighbouring Uganda experienced through the years especially in the northern part of the country which was devastated by violence that was partly caused by ethnic rivalries, there is no question that it also has had its share of bloodshed caused by ethnic conflicts.

In fact, Kenya has witnessed some of the worst forms of violence in East Africa in contemporary times.

The bloodiest conflicts took place in the 1990s between different ethnic groups and, in many cases, the violence was politically motivated, ignited and fuelled by unscrupulous politicians.

But the violence was also sparked by pure hatred and xenophobic fear among some people, especially in the Coast and Rift Valley Provinces, who resented members of other tribes from other parts of Kenya who had moved into and settled in those regions.

Many of the "outsiders" or "foreigners" who were

attacked had lived there for years. And a very large number of them were also born in those provinces, the only place they knew as home.

They also, of course, had the right to live there as Kenyans themselves. But that is not how the indigenous people saw them. They saw them as "strangers," "foreigners," "outsiders," and as "invaders" who had gone there to displace the "rightful" owners of the land and were not welcome. Anything that could be done to expel them - had to be done. And that included killing them. It became an orgy of killings.

It was one of the most tragic chapters in Kenya's history. And what happened then continues to haunt the nation today, as it continues its precarious existence simply because the leaders themselves - not all but a significant number of them - show that they are no more concerned about ending tribal rivalries than an ordinary person is; a person who is motivated by ethnic hatred towards fellow Kenyans for no other reason than that they don't belong to his or her tribe.

A large number of leaders are tribalist, favouring members of their own tribes. And they exploit ethnic and regional differences and rivalries in their quest for power and to perpetuate themselves in office. That is what happened in the 1990s. And it could happened again.

Back in the early 1990s, the ruling party KANU dominated by the Kalenjin from the Rift Valley Province – under the leadership of President Danie arap Moi who was a Kalenjin himself – played a major role in igniting the violence between different ethnic groups which almost tore the country apart in order to consolidate its position and stay in power. The result was bloodshed the country had never seen since Mau Mau.

At least 3,000 people were killed or severely wounded in the Rift Valley Province alone in 1992.

The primary target were the Kikuyu and other "foreigners" - Kenyans from other provinces - who had settled in the Rift Valley Province. The Kikuyu, who had moved and settled there in large numbers, suffered the most.

The attacks were carried out by the Kalenjin, members of President Moi's ethnic group which is dominant in the region. And nothing was done to the perpetrators of this violence.

Only a few years later before the presidential election in 1997, the Coast Province was the scene of the same kind of violence. The people who were killed were mostly "outsiders" who came from other parts of Kenya and settled in the Coast Province.

Leaflets written in Kiswahili were distributed in the region urging the indigenous people to drive out the "invaders" from other provinces. According to the *International Herald* Tribune, 18 August 1997, some of the leaflets stated: "The time has come for us original inhabitants of the coast to claim what is rightfully ours. We must remove these invaders from our land."

The people who were attacked came from the interior. They were mostly Kikuyu, Luo, Luhya, Kamba and others who had settled in the Coast Province. One witness in Mombasa, Edmund Kwena, was quoted by the *International Herald Tribune* saying a filling station was attacked and a pump set on fire.

He also said he saw scores of buildings torched on 17 August 1997, four days after the violence erupted in the Coast Province. He went on to say: "I personally counted up to 100 kiosks completely burned down. Dozens of houses were also set on fire in the Diani area, a popular tourist area south of Mombasa."

The preceding statements are cited in Godfrey Mwakikagile, *Ethnic Politics in Kenya and Nigeria* (pp. 120 - 121), a comparative study.

The ruling Kenya African National Union (KANU) under President Moi - which was dominated by the Kalenjin and their allies who were also mainly members of smaller tribes like the Kalenjin themselves - was accused of instigating the violence. The main target were members of tribes opposed to Moi's despotic rule. These were mostly Kikuyu, Luo, Luhya, Kamba and others.

The attacks were reminiscent of what had taken place in other African counties where members of tribes who were not considered to be original inhabitants of the regions they had migrated to were killed or expelled from those regions where many of them had lived for decades.

The attacks in the Rift Valley and Coast Provinces in Kenya and the inflammatory language used by the instigators of this kind of violence to inflame passions among the indigenous people in those provinces had striking similarities to what happened in Nigeria in the sixties and in Zaire in the early nineties:

The language had striking parallels to what Northern Nigerian leaders said about the Igbos who had settled in their region. As Representative Mallam Mukhtar Bello stated in the Northern House of Assembly during the February-March 1964 session just two years before the massacre of the Igbos in that region:

'I would like to say something very important that the Minister should take my appeal to the Federal Government (controlled by Northerners) about the Igbos....I wish the number of these Igbos be reduced....There are too many of them in the North. They are just like sardines and I think they are just too dangerous to the Region.'

The rest of the representatives in the Northern Regional Assembly expressed the same sentiment, including the Northern Premier himself, Sir Ahmadu Bello.

This hostility exploded into violence almost exactly two years later against the Igbos who had settled in the Northern Region. Most of them had lived there for decades.

And almost exactly 30 years later, the same thing happened in the Coast Province of Kenya against the people who came from the interior; and in Zaire (now the Democratic Republic of Congo) in 1993 when President Mobutu Sese Seko employed the same tactic against his opponents, igniting tribal violence which led to the massacre of thousands of people from Kasai Province who had settled in Shaba Province (formerly Katanga Province).

They also had lived there for decades, and their home province, Kasai, was also the home region of Mobutu's most powerful and influential rival, Etienne Tshisekedi.

Like the Igbos in Northern Nigeria, and the Kikuyu, the Luo, the Luhya, the Kamba and members of other tribes from inland who had settled in Kenya's Coast Province, the people from Kasai Province were also expelled *en masse* from Shaba Province.

And in all three cases, murder was the primary weapon used to facilitate the expulsion of these 'outsiders' and 'invaders.' - (Godfrey Mwakikagile, *Ethnic Politics in Kenya and Nigeria* (Huntington, New York: Nova Science Publishers, Inc.,), p. 120; the expulsion of Igbos from Northern Nigeria also cited in *Africa Contemporary Record* (London, 1969), p. 664).

Kenyan newspapers were quick to report the violence in the Coast Province and stated that the attacks in that region appeared to be similar to those which took place in the Rift Valley Province before and after the general election in 1992.

There was unmistakable evidence of ethnic hostility which ignited and fuelled the violence. At least 1,500 Kikuyus and members of other tribes – but mostly Kikuyus - who had settled in the Rift Valley province were killed. Their property was also destroyed. As Gibson Kuria, a renowned human rights lawyer who was active in the movement for constitutional reforms, stated:

This looks too much like 1992. The violence is aimed at certain ethnic communities, the government response has been lukewarm, and the violence we're seeing has had the same kind of brutality. - (Quoted by Godfrey Mwakikagile, *Ethnic Politics in Kenya and Nigeria*, ibid., p. 121; also, cited by G. Mwakikagile, "Explosion of Violence in Kenya Stirs Fears of Electoral Mayhem," in the *International Herald Tribune*, 21 August 1997, p. 6).

When the attacks were launched, no one knew what the outcome would be. There were tens of thousands of Kikuyus, Luos, Kambas, Merus, Luhyas and members of other inland tribes who had lived in the Coast Province for decades and knew no other place as home. They were well-established in the region and no one would have expected them to pack up and leave just like that. And it seemed that the majority of them were going to stay. But that is not what happened in many cases.

Marauding gangs of between 200 and 500 indigenous people, native to the Coast, attacked these "foreigners" and "invaders" indiscriminately, determined to force them to go back where they came from. And they succeeded in driving them out of many areas.

They used all kinds of weapons including guns, clubs with nails, machetes, and bows and arrows. They also used arson as a major weapon. According to the *International Herald Tribune*:

They burned homes and businesses and hacked off people's limbs....Signs of tension are everywhere. Trucks bounce along, stuffed with fleeing families' belongings (going back upcountry). - (cited by Godfrey Mwakikagile, *Ethnic Politics in Kenya and Nigeria*, p. 121).

The government denied involvement but there was incontrovertible evidence showing that it was indeed behind the violence.

In fact, some of the irrefutable evidence came from the government itself and its ruling party officials based on what they said in public on different occasions before this politically motivated ethnic violence - fuelled by xenophobia - erupted. Even the police, to fool and impress the public, arrested one KANU activist involved in the violence – yet did nothing to stop it:

Thus far, police have arrested at least one KANU activist in connection with the unrest....

In recent months several ruling party politicians have exhorted indigenous Mombasans to force outside groups back up country. - (*International Herald Tribune*, and Godfrey Mwakikagile, ibid.).

The fears opponents of Moi's regime had expressed were now justified. They accused the ruling party, KANU, of using violence to consolidate the president's position just before the general election and burnish his image in the Coast Province by expelling from the region members of ethnic groups such as the Kikuyu and Luo opposed to his tribalistic and autocratic rule. As Richard Leakey, a Kenyan of British origin born in Kenya who was one of Moi's most vocal critics, bluntly stated:

There is no doubt that there is a political agenda in scaring the hell out of the upcountry people. - (Quoted by the *International Herald Tribune*, 21 August 1997, p. 6, and by Godfrey Mwakikagile, *Ethnic Politics in Kenya and Nigeria*, op. cit, p. 122).

And the violence continued. At the Likoni Catholic Church, about 3,000 people from upcountry who were members of the Kikuyu, Kamba, Luo and other tribes, filled the compound. They brought with them all their possessions or whatever they could carry or get the chance to take, with their enemies in hot pursuit.

It was a gruesome sight. They had been slashed with machetes, shot or severely beaten by some of the members of the Coastal tribes.

One of the victims was Jeremiah Mwindi Muli, 38 years old, and he had a harrowing tale of what happened to him.

He was returning home one morning from a nearby shop when he was attacked. About 20 young men armed with guns, clubs and machetes confronted him in an alley. They asked him for some money. Then they asked him what tribe he was. He told them he was a Kamba. And they attacked him.

He ran but they caught up with him and slashed him on both shoulders and on his upper right arm. His arm was paralysed from the attack.

After he returned to his house, everything was gone. He and his wife, Kanini, had two sons, one 5 years old, and the other one, only 18 months. Now they had nothing, not even clothes except the ones they had on:

They even took our spoons. I'm poor and displaced, and I've lost all my possessions. I don't know how I'll start again. - (Quoted, ibid.).

The violence triggered an exodus never witnessed in the country's history on such a scale:

Residents estimated that at least 40,000 of the total population of 60,000 had left the Kwale district since the start of ethnic attacks by gangs on August 13.

Throughout the night, men, women and children clutching a few belongings left homes and walked to bus and railway stations. - (*International Herald Tribune*, 30 August 1997, cited by Godfrey Mwakikagile, *Ethnic Politics in Kenya and Nigeria*, ibid., p. 123).

That was from one area alone. People from the hinterland had settled all over the Coast Province, and there was no place in the region where they felt safe.

Tens of thousands of other upcountry people fled from all over the Coast province within the same week of the attacks and in subsequent days, vowing never to return. It was one of the saddest chapters in the nation's history.

The exodus was reminiscent of what happened to the Igbos when they fled from Northern Nigeria and returned to their home region in Eastern Nigeria after they were attacked and tens of thousands of their compatriots were massacred in the North in 1966. At least 50,000 were killed in a few weeks.

Kenya in the 1990s was divided along ethnic lines as much as Nigeria was in the late sixties in terms of violence; the difference was in the magnitude of the violence – it was worse in Nigeria, and more people were killed there. But the hostility was the same, nonetheless. And the same problem exists in both countries today as much as it does in most African countries.

In Kenya, the outcome of the December 1997 presidential election was not surprising. Moi won by playing the ethnic card. As one western diplomat said about Moi's victory and support for his ruling Kenya African National Union (KANU) by small tribes:

That's not surprising when you consider that KANU is an alliance of small tribes whose main priority is preventing the Luos or the Kikuyus from taking power. - (Quoted by *The Christian Science Monitor*, 6 January 1998, p. 6, and Godfrey Mwakikagile, *Ethnic Politics in Kenya and Nigeria*, ibid., p. 137).

Before Moi became president and filled the ruling party with members of his tribe, the Kalenjin, and of other small tribes allied with the Kalenjin, KANU was dominated by the Kikuyu under the leadership of their patriarch Jomo Kenyatta.

Other tribes resented that and were determined it would never happen again. It may not have, but the problem remained the same: power concentrated in the hands of one or a few ethnic groups, this time the Kalenjin and their allies, to the exclusion of the rest.

And even after the 1997 general election, the violence continued. The Kalenjin and their allies including the Maasai had won again, and consolidated their position, and felt that they could do anything they wanted to do at the expense of others – the Kikuyu, the Luo, the Luhya, the Kamba – without fear of retribution or legal sanctions since they were in power. They dominated and controlled the government under Moi, the most prominent and most powerful Kalenjin in the history of that tribe in modern times.

And they turned their home region, the Rift Valley Province, into a combat zone for ethnic cleansing.

The fighting, and killings, had already been going on in the Rift Valley Province even before the election and during the same time the violence was also going on in the Coast Province against non-indigenes. In fact, it happened even earlier.

Thousands of people who were displaced in 1991 during the ethnic attacks against the Kikuyu and others had neither returned nor received any help from Moi's government.

The Rift Valley Province was forbidden territory for them, although it been their home before the violence in the early 1990s. The violence perpetrated against them was justified – by the Kalenjins and their allies – solely on the grounds that they were not Kalenjin or native to the region, and did not support President Daniel arap Moi, a Kalenjin.

Three weeks after Moi was sworn in as president in January 1998, the violence continued to take its toll:

Raiders armed with automatic rifles, bows and arrows, and spears have killed 22 more people in central Kenya, police said yesterday (January 27, 1998), raising the death toll in politically motivated violence this month to 77.

The latest violence broke out near the farming town of Njoro, where assailants have killed 22 people since Sunday (January 25), police spokesman Peter Kimathi said. 23 people were wounded....

The attacks apparently are aimed at driving Kenya's biggest tribe, the Kikuyu, off their land in the Rift Valley Province because they voted against President Daniel arap Moi's Kenya African National Union party in the December 29 – 30 elections.

Earlier this month, two of Moi's cabinet ministers openly threatened Kikuyu residents of the province in speeches at a rally of the Kenya African National Union party to celebrate their electoral victory.

Observers of the latest attack say the assailants were members of the Kalenjin group of tribes, which generally support Moi. - (*The Boston Globe*, 28 January 1998, and Godfrey Mwakikagile, *Ethnic Politics in Kenya and Nigeria*, ibid., p. 138).

In 1992 and 1993, similar violence in the Rift Valley Province wreaked havoc on an unprecedented scale. About 2,000 people were killed, and 300,000 displaced. Most of them were Kikuyus.

What happened then is not just history. It is a perennial problem in terms of ethnic relations.

Different tribes still don't trust each other. They don't even like each other. Some do, some don't, as individuals. But as ethnic groups, the chasm runs deep. And nothing has been done to close it.

The ethnic violence in Kenya in the 1990s may be a thing of the past, but it is very much a part of the present. Ethnic tensions are an enduring phenomenon in Kenyan national life. And they erupted into violence a decade ago.

It happened then, and it could happen again. It is up to the people and the leaders to make sure that it doesn't happen again.

Tanzania is the only country in the region, if not on the entire continent, that has virtually conquered tribalism and racism. Even many foreigners who have been to Tanzania and other African countries have noticed that.

One of them was Keith B. Richburg, a black American journalist who was the bureau chief of *The Washington Post* in Nairobi for three years. As he states in his book – whose candour has inflamed passions among many people, especially black Americans and Africans – *Out of America: A Black Man Confronts Africa*:

Moi became more thorough in his consolidation of power, placing loyal tribesmen in key government posts and cracking down hard on his perceived enemies within....

Even in a relatively modern state like Kenya, tribal animosities bubble just an inch beneath the surface.

The Kikuyu are the largest tribe and until Moi took over, had been at the forefront of the country's independence struggles and its early postcolonial politics. Jomo Kenyatta was a Kikuyu, and he was by all accounts a particularly harsh autocrat, a tribal chieftain of the first order who believed it was the Kikuyu's natural right to rule.

Many Kenyans, non-Kikuyu, are deathly fearful of another Kikuyu presidency (although they later voted for Mwai Kibaki, a Kikuyu, to succeed Moi), and Moi has managed to tap into that fear and present himself as the only alternative. Moi has likewise been willing to allow more than a few tribal eruptions to make his point to Kenya and the world – that he alone represents stability for Kenya, that without him the country becomes just another African tribal killing zone....

164

If there was one thing I learned traveling around Africa, it was that the tribe remains the defining feature of almost every African society. Old tribal mistrusts and stereotypes linger, and the potential for a violent implosion is never very far from the surface.

Even in the supposedly more sophisticated or developed countries like Kenya, thirty years of independence and "nation building" had still failed to create any real sense of national identity that could transcend the tribe.

In Kenya, the Kikuyu still think the Luo are inferior and that they, the Kikuyu, have the right to rule. The Luo don't trust the Kikuyu, who they think look down on them. And both tribes look down on the Luhya. It goes on and on.

In Kenya, I also saw the devastating effects of what can happen when politicians, like Danie arap Moi and his cronies, are willing to play the "tribal card" and stoke the flames of ethnic animosity for political advantage.

I walked through the burned-out town of Enosupukio, after it was raided by Masai warriors driving out (the) Kikuyu who they believed had settled on traditional Masai grazing land. It looked like a war zone after a major battle, which, in a way, I suppose it was.

Not a single house or shop was left standing. Even two churches were stripped of everything except a few pews. And when I spoke to the Kikuyu refugees who had fled the town, they told me how the Masai who had once been their neighbors suddenly swooped down on the town with guns and machetes and spears.

One woman named Loyce Majiru told me how she had to flee with her nine children, and how she looked back and saw the body of a neighbor on the side of the road, naked, with his head chopped off.

And this was Kenya, a major tourist destination and a country long considered one of the more "stable" in Africa.

These things, though, are not too popular to discuss outside of Africa, particularly among the Africanists and Western academics for whom the very term "tribe" is anathema. The preferred term is "ethnic group" because it's considered less racially laden. But Africans themselves talk of their "tribes," and they warn of the potential for tribal explosion...." - (Keith B. Richburg, *Out of America: A Black Man Confronts Africa* (New York: Basic Books), pp. 25 – 26, 104 - 105).

Richburg goes on to talk about his experience in Kenya and other African countries and about the devastating impact of tribalism:

I remember first arriving in Kenya and going to see one of those old colonial Brits, a man named Douglas – I never knew his first name – who worked in a cramped, dingy, smoke-stained office above the souvenir shop, surrounded by stacks and stacks of paper files in blue and pink and yellow cardboard folders.

He was a large man with white hair and a thick white mustache, and his suspenders pulled his pants so high up his waist they looked like they were touching his armpits. He was the real estate agent for the house I was renting, and I had to go to his office to drop off my check.

And I remember him sitting back imperiously with his hands over his wide stomach and appraising me, the newcomer to Africa, and then announcing, "You Americans don't know anything about the African. It's all tribes – tribes! And you don't understand that." And I recall thinking at the time, how pompous this old man was, how utterly full of himself, bandying about that old worn cliche, tribalism, to explain Africa's ills.

I set out to prove old Douglas wrong. One of my earliest visits was to Tanzania, and there I found a country that had actually managed to purge itself of the evil of tribalism.

Under Julius Nyerere and his ruling socialists, the government was able to imbue a true sense of nationalism that transcended the country's natural ethnic divisions, among other things by vigorous campaigns to upgrade education and to make Swahili a truly national language.

Swahili today is widely spoken everywhere and has become the medium of instruction at Tanzanian universities, where I met a professor of Swahili studies who was busy translating the latest American computer program into Swahili.

Tanzania is one place that has succeeded in removing the linguistic barrier that separates so many of Africa's warring factions.

But after three years traveling the continent, I've found that Tanzania is the exception, not the rule. In Africa, as old man Douglas said, it is all about tribes.

Tribalism is what prompted tens of thousands of Rwandan Hutus to pick up machetes and hoes and panga knives and farming tools to bash in the skulls and sever the limbs of their Tutsi neighbors. Tribalism is why entire swaths of Kenya's scenic Rift Valley lie in scorched ruins, why Zulu gunmen in ski masks mow down Xhosa workers outside a factory gate in South Africa, and why thousands of hungry displaced Kasai huddle under plastic sheeting at a remote train station in eastern Zaire.

And it's tribalism under another name – clans, subclans, factions – that caused young men in Mogadishu to shell the city to oblivion and loot what was left of the rubble. - (K.B. Richburg, ibd., pp. 240 - 241).

There may even be a few other African countries, in fact very few if there are indeed any other, that are free from the scourge of tribalism and racism - in virulent form - like Tanzania is.

Botswana is one of them but probably because it is composed almost entirely of members of one ethnic group, the Tswana, besides the so-called Bushmen of the Kalahari desert many of whom may have an entirely different story to tell about their treatment at the hands of the dominant ethnic group.

In fact, there are many complaints which have been reported through the years – by "Bushmen" and their supporters – about the mistreatment of these indigenous people by the Tswana-dominated government. According to one report, "Rights Group Likens Bushmen Plight to Slavery," by *Voice of America (VOA) Africa News,* 23 August 2007:

The human rights group Survival International released a new report Thursday (23 August 2007) comparing the situation of Botswana's Bushmen to the trans-Atlantic slave trade.

The report is being issued to mark the UN Day for the Remembrance of the Slave Trade and its Abolition.

The report says the same arguments used to defend slavery "bear a striking similarity" to those used to justify the eviction of the Bushmen from their ancestral lands.

The Gana and Gwi Bushmen were relocated from the Central Kalahari Game Reserve in 2002. Last December, they won a court case to return to their lands.

However, the government says only those named in the lawsuit, several hundred, should be allowed to return. Those who have returned accuse the government of preventing them from hunting, bringing in goats or using a nearby borehole for water.

Survival International Director Stephen Corry says there's a worldwide prejudice against "tribal and indigenous people."

"It's very clear that there's an attitude that they are somehow inferior, that they need to catch up, that they are uncivilized. They need to be civilized. And this is exactly the same thing which was said about the slave trade 200 years ago. I mean I think it is very easy to forget that the slave trade had a lot of defenders. People who were arguing that it benefited and helped civilize Africans. And that's a direct quote from somebody in 1774," he says.

Corry says that the government is using old arguments in its relocation of the Bushmen.

"The Botswanan government thinks their way of life is inferior. It sees them as hunter-gatherers, who should stop being hunter-gatherers and should, as it were, join the mainstream of society," he says.

The Botswanan government has said the Bushmen would benefit by leaving game reserve by having better access to water, social and educational services.

A government document says a fund has been set up to provide training and help for Bushmen who want to start small businesses.

The government also says it wants to raise their standard of living and avoid land-use conflicts in the Central Kalahari Game Reserve as a result of agriculture and livestock.

Corry says the quality of life and health of the relocated Bushmen has deteriorated sharply. He says that you cannot use force to relocate indigenous people "without damaging them very severely."

"Wherever there are tribal peoples still living in a way which they wish to live, the dominant societies often regard it as inferior and want to stop it, not least and generally because they want their land. That's what it usually boils down to," he says.

The Botswanan government, however, is quoted as saying it wants to bring the Bushmen into "the mainstream society without any detriment to their unique culture and tradition."

The country's foreign minister was quoted in 2001 as saying, "It would be grossly irresponsible if we didn't expose them to modern day culture."

If the "Bushmen" are indeed discriminated against and are seen as inferior to the Tswana, then that's tribalism and ethnic prejudice against these indigenous people.

So, Tanzania may still be the exception on the whole continent as a country that has virtually conquered tribalism. And in a few others also, such as Swaziland and may be even Namibia (that's may be), tribalism may not be a major problem like in Kenya, Rwanda, Burundi, Nigeria and other countries across the continent, although there have been some complaints against the Ovambo, Namibia's dominant ethnic group.

Also, there have been some complaints now and then against the Chaga, the Haya, and the Nyakyusa (my tribe) in Tanzania who, for decades since independence, have had a disproportionately large number of jobs requiring high education.

But that is mainly for historical reasons. They had the opportunity to go school - members of other tribes did not have in large numbers - during colonial rule because they were mostly Christian and attended schools founded by missionaries in their home districts and regions; a point also underscored by President Nyerere when he heard some people complain that members of these three tribes had most of the jobs requiring high education. They wrongly attributed that to tribalism, a complaint Nyerere dismissed as unfounded.

There is no question that there are tribalists among them, including some in my tribe, the Nyakyusa; this is not a world of angels, but of human beings, with our own weaknesses and prejudices. And there will always be such people in all tribes. But, in spite of all that, tribalism still has never been a major problem in Tanzania. It has been effectively contained or neutralised in most areas of national life.

What Tanzania has achieved is not a miracle. Others can do it.

In fact, one of the reasons - besides economic inequities among the member states of the East African Community (EAC) dominated by Kenya, and other factors - many Tanzanians were adamantly opposed to fast-tracking the process of forming an East African political federation was their well-founded fear that tribalism in neighbouring countries like Kenya would spread to Tanzania like cancer and threaten the peace and stability the country has enjoyed since independence, if the countries were to unite under one government.

Tanzanians, of all races, are just people like any other human beings. They are not angels. They did not come from another planet. They are not endowed with any special qualities other Africans – or any other people on planet Earth – don't have. If they can conquer, or effectively contain, tribalism and racism to the point where these twin evils are not a major problem in national life, there is no reason why Kenyans can't do it.

And why not the rest across the continent? As Julius Nyerere used to say about nation building, which includes fighting and eliminating tribalism and racism, "It can be done, play your part."

Chapter Eight:

Kenya in Contemporary Times

TO MANY casual observers, Kenya is a peaceful and relatively prosperous country. People get along just fine, the economy bounces along, and the future looks bright.

It is even seen as an island of stability in a turbulent region – with the exception of Tanzania, of course, which for decades has been a haven for refugees from neighbouring countries which are now and then mired in conflict.

But that is not the whole story about Kenya. Yes, it is peaceful and prosperous, relatively speaking, and it is the most developed and richest country in East Africa. Yet, there are problems, a lot of problems, in this land of prosperity. And they are major, not minor, problems.

Beneath all that façade, there are simmering tensions between different ethnic and interest groups. There is also a lot of poverty. The rich continue to get richer, and the poor remain poor or get poorer.

Structural adjustment programmes and other austerity measures recommended and imposed by the World Bank and it sister institution the International Monetary Fund (IMF), and by donor nations, on poor countries to fuel economic growth, have not benefited the poor.

Little has trickled down. Only the elite benefit, fuelling hostility among the masses towards the vampire class. And that applies to all developing countries, not just Kenya.

Corruption is endemic. And Western countries themselves, who are the biggest donors, condone it or do very little to help combat it.

Money stolen by corrupt officials and unscrupulous politicians and businessmen – and businesswomen – is spirited out of the country and stashed away in banks in Western countries with the full knowledge of Western governments and, in many cases, in collusion with corrupt officials and businessmen – and businesswomen – in those countries.

Billions of dollars are stolen every year, and Kenya ranks high, in fact very high, among African countries many of whose leaders and other powerful people steal billions of dollars every year and deposit the loot abroad. It's not their money.

Attempts to bring about fundamental change have been made. And the people continue trying. Yet they are divided among themselves. They are divided along tribal and regional lines. Even many interest groups are regionally entrenched. The coalitions they form, in order to work together, are only temporary. They don't last long, a weakness those in power exploit to perpetuate themselves in office.

Those in office don't even hide what they do. They are brazen. They practise tribalism openly, and they steal without any fear of being punished.

While Kenyans worked together and transcended tribal and regional loyalties to form a coalition which swept the Kenya African National Union (KANU) out of power after ruling the country since independence in 1963, they failed to continue working together effectively without ethno-regional biases.

The coalition was only temporary and it fragmented along ethnic and regional lines to satisfy the political ambitions of individual leaders lusting for power to advance their own personal - and tribal as well as regional - agendas.

Different coalitions of ethno-regional and interest groups were formed. They were also bound to collapse, without any hope that out of the ruins would emerge truly national parties transcending ethnic and regional loyalties and interests.

Although the country is divided along ethnic and regional lines, there are many things which the people of different tribes have in common besides their shared identity as Kenyans.

The majority of Kenyans are farmers. Agriculture is practised by members of many different tribes. That's one of the things many different tribes – from the Luo to the Kikuyu, the Kamba to the Luhya – have in common.

There are also a number of tribes whose members are pastoralists. The Maasai are the most well-known in this category. But even those who lead sedentary lives as farmers have livestock like the Maasai do. They include the Kikuyu and the Kamba. There are also pastoralists who are farmers. There are, for example, Maasai who are engaged in agriculture.

Therefore pastoralist tribes have a lot in common with agriculturalists in terms of economic activities. They do the same things to earn a living; not all of them, but a significant number of them do. There was indeed a time when almost all Maasais engaged in pastoralism. That is not the case anymore.

Then you have urban dwellers. They come from all tribes. That is another very important thing they have in common which also has helped to break down tribal barriers in a number of cases because of tribal intermingling and even intermarriage, especially among the young and the educated.

The standard of living of Kenyans living in cities and towns is usually higher than that of their counterparts in most African countries. But there has been a decline in the quality of life in recent years attributed to economic problems, including the inability of the economy to absorb all those seeking employment. Here is an example to illustrate this point.

In 1997, some Kenyan leaders including President Danile arap Moi said there were no jobs and even encouraged many young people who were unemployed – many of them with college degrees – to leave Kenya and look for jobs in other countries.

There were no jobs for them in their own country. College graduates with degrees in accountancy had to haul bricks and sacks of maize to earn a living in Nairobi and other parts of the country.

In fact many Kenyans had been leaving Kenya every year even before then, never to return. They still do so today. Thousands leave every year. In the United States alone, there are more than 40,000 highly educated Kenyans, including professionals practically in all fields, who probably have no intention of returning home.

Many Kenyans leave for a number of reasons: lack of employment, low wages and salaries, poor working conditions, bureaucratic interference especially for professionals, lack of freedom, and a deteriorating economy, prompting some people to recall with nostalgia the "good old days" of British colonial rule.

It is not a majority sentiment but the mere fact that there are some people who would even entertain such an idea is disturbing. As Kenyan human rights lawyer and political activist Njonjo Mue said in a speech at a conference of Kenyans living abroad in St. Paul, Minnesota, USA, in July 2000: "I have heard intelligent people ask, 'If only the British would come back and colonize us!'"

It is a sentiment of despair and desperation. And it explains why so many people, especially of the younger generation, have lost faith in government and no longer trust their leaders.

The society remains stratified, and the nature of economic activities remains basically the same but without much hope for the vast majority of the people to escape poverty. They are trapped. Yet they continue to survive against overwhelming odds.

Kenya is a typical Third World country and there are basically three major categories of Kenyans in terms of economic activities: farmers, pastoralists, and urban residents who earn their living working in towns and cities. And we may add another category, that of fishermen. They live along the coast of the Indian Ocean, in towns and villages, and on the shores of Lake Victoria as well as near or around other freshwater lakes in different parts of the country.

Urban dwellers call Nairobi, Mombasa and other towns and cities - home. That's the only place many of them have known as their home. They were born and brought up there. But they are not the only residents of those urban areas.

Others include those who have moved to towns and cities from the rural areas in search of jobs. That is their new home. But they have not severed ties with their people in the countryside.

Many urban dwellers still maintain strong ties with their traditional homes and families in villages in rural areas across Kenya.

But there are also those who have practically severed ties with traditional Africa and don't even know or speak their tribal languages. Usually, these are the ones who were born and brought up in towns or cities or have lived in urban areas for so long that they have forgotten their tribal languages, and know very little about their tribal customs and traditions But they are a minority.

A much higher percentage of Kenyans living in cities and towns speak their tribal languages, know their tribal customs and traditions, and maintain ties with their people in their tribal homelands. They even have tribal associations to help each other in times of need and crisis, or simply to participate in social functions including weddings. They also take trips to see their people in the rural areas and even help them financially.

That is typical Africa.

You can take tribesmen out of the village but you can't take the village out of them. And that is true in a very large number of cases even among the most educated and most cosmopolitan.

The cosmopolitan nature of the capital itself, Nairobi, is very much indicative of Kenya's status in the regional context.

Kenya is unquestionably the economic powerhouse not only of East Africa – which usually means Kenya, Uganda, and Tanzania – but of the entire Eastern Africa which includes the Horn of Africa: Somalia, Ethiopia, Eritrea and Djibouti.

Kenya's infrastructural development including expansion of education all the way to the university level since independence has been impressive. And the country continues to grow, although the former sleeping giant next-door, Tanzania, which slumbered for years during the socialist era under *ujamaa* (the country's African version of socialism) that stunted economic growth, now poses a serious challenge to Kenya as the prime mover in the region.

Even during colonial times, Tanzania – what was then Tanganyika – was known as the Cinderella of East Africa. But not anymore. That was then. Today, with its abundant natural resources including a dazzling array of minerals (and probably large quantities of oil deposits), Tanzania is destined to be the economic giant of the entire region of Eastern Africa in years to come.

But until then, Kenya will continue to rule the region in terms of economic might. And the evidence is everywhere when compared with her neighbours.

Kenyan schools are better; its transport system is much more developed; and so are medical services and many other things across a wide range of the social and economic spectrum.

Visitors to Nairobi have plenty to see. The city has all the evidence of a bustling metropolis, at least by African standards, in an underdeveloped region. And it has all the social amenities one expects in a modern city in developed countries. It is also a city that blends the traditional with the modern, giving it a unique flavour among Africa's largest and most cosmopolitan cities.

And the country as a whole is relatively stable, again at least by African standards on a continent mired in conflict and characterised by political instability. But the tranquil atmosphere is deceptive. That's only on the surface.

Underneath is a strong undercurrent of ethnic and regional sentiments which threaten national unity. The way people vote is one of the best examples of that. Employment is another example where almost entire departments are filled by members of one tribe as long as their tribesmen, or kinsmen, are on top, or in charge.

But let's look at one example, elections, in which people vote for candidates, not because they believe they are the best to lead the country; not because of their political and ideological interests but because the candidates they vote for are members of their tribes.

And at no time in Kenyan history since independence has this been more apparent than it is today, in contemporary times, especially since the introduction of multi-party democracy in the early nineties.

The first multi-party election clearly showed the power of ethnic alliances, tipping scales in favour of the incumbent, President Danie arap Moi, who mobilised tribes and candidates allied with his Kalenjin ethnic community into a formidable political force.

Subsequent elections were equally marred by tribal loyalties. In the 1992 and 1997 presidential elections, each major tribe - except the Kisii who did not field a presidential candidate - voted for its own candidate. The Kikuyu, Kenya's largest, overwhelmingly voted for Mwai Kibaki; the Luo for Raila Odinga, son of former Vice President Oginga Odinga under Jomo Kenyatta; the Luhya for Kijana Wamalwa; and the Kamba for Mrs. Charity Ngilu.

They all lost, of course, because of tribalism among themselves and kept in power an unabashedly tribalistic president whose government was dominated by his fellow Kalenjin tribesmen. As Mrs. Charity Ngilu, a member of the fourth-largest tribe in Kenya, the Kamba, who was also the first woman in Kenyan history to be a serious contender for the presidency in the 1997 general election, lamented after the election which the incumbent Daniel arap Moi easily won because the opposition was hopelessly divided along tribal lines and failed to rally behind a single candidate:

Honourable Mwai Kibaki got most votes in 1997 from the Kikuyu, Honourable Raila Odinga from the Luo, Honourable Kijana Wamalwa from the Luhya and I myself from the Kamba. President Moi got most of his votes from the Rift Valley. Is this the Kenya we want? - (Charity Ngilu, speaking in Bokoli village, Bungoma, Kenya, January 8, 2000, quoted by Kenyan Professor Kivutha Kibwana, "Ethnic Politics: Curse or Blessing," Nairobi, Kenya, July 2001, in Godfrey Mwakikagile, *Nyerere and Africa: End of an Era*, 2nd edition (Las Vegas, Nevada, USA: Protea Publishing), p. 43).

The politics of ethnic solidarity went even further during the 2007 presidential campaign and election when the leader of a major opposition party (KANU) who was a Kikuyu endorsed the incumbent, Mwai Kibaki, who was also a Kikuyu. And both came from the same place, the Central Province, a Kikuyu stronghold; it is, in fact, the traditional homeland of the Kikuyu.

The leader of the opposition who endorsed Mwai Kibaki was Uhuru Kenyatta, son of Kenya's first president,

Jomo Kenyatta. Uhuru Kenyatta was also KANU's presidential candidate in the 2000 general election. And his endorsement of President Mwai Kibaki for a second term was widely condemned by the media and other segments of the Kenyan society.

It was a clear-cut case of tribalism. Tribalism was a major factor in the endorsement, if it wasn't *the* major factor. Kibaki's new coalition party was known as PANU (Party of National Unity) and, like KANU, was also dominated by the Kikuyu but faced a formidable challenge from Raila Odinga, a Luo, who had some success in mobilising forces across ethno-regional lines in a country still dominated by ethnic loyalties.

"BBC Africa," in its report of 17 September 2007 entitled "Kenyan Press Slams Ethnic Politics," published on its web site the following comments - a sample - from Kenyan newspapers on the subject tribalism, a cancer that is gradually destroying the country:

> What, at the moment, seems to matter, is the ethnicity of the three contenders - one reason Kenyans keep voting for the wrong people and sidelining those who would bring fresh thinking into politics. - editorial in the *Daily Nation*.

> Kanu Chairman Mr Uhuru Kenyatta [leader of the post-independence party Kenya African National Union] is reluctant to stand against President Kibaki out of ethnic considerations... The gesture could as well seal the fate of Kanu, a party that ruled the country for 40 years. - Mutula Kilonzo in the *Standard*.

Yet, destructive as it is, ethnicity is the bedrock upon which African societies - including modern states – are founded. And it explains why they are so fragile and so unstable, in spite of their image and reputation as functional entities, relatively speaking.

Kenya is a typical example of that. It has been relatively stable for decades since independence. Yet, it is threatened from within, although it has not yet been torn apart, by ethnic rivalries.

And it is not just at the presidential level that ethnicity has manifested itself in its virulent form during election campaigns. The contest for parliamentary seats has been equally divisive.

Ethnic sentiments were very much alive during campaigns for parliamentary seats, running parallel to quest for votes by presidential candidates on the basis of ethnic and regional loyalties. In fact, in 2007, Kenya's media expressed grave concern about ethnic sentiments creeping into the body politic ahead of the December presidential and parliamentary elections.

And it was clear that many of the presidential aspirants were also appointing various running mates largely based on which ethnic grouping would give them the largest number of votes in the coming general elections, and not on the basis of political agendas and manifestoes.

Ethnic alliances became a formidable force in the election. For example, the Luo and the Luhya – backing presidential candidate Raila Odinga, a Luo – formed an alliance against the Kikuyu and their allies, especially the Embu and the Meru, who supported incumbent Mwai Kibaki, a Kikuyu, for another presidential term.

In other words, different tribes and ethnic blocs or coalitions were competing for power at the national level and voting against other tribes and regions, not as fellow countrymen for their collective well-being, and not for leaders who would unite them and lead Kenya as one country; they were voting to benefit themselves on tribal and regional basis at the expense of other tribes and regions.

But it was also clear that among all the candidates, Raila Odinga transcended ethnicity in terms of appeal and got support from many parts of the country, because of his agenda, his credentials as a populist, and also because he was running against an incumbent who had not fulfilled his major promises since he went into office; although it was also equally clear that Odinga himself had overwhelming support among his fellow tribesmen, the Luo in his home province of Nyanza which was also his political stronghold, and among their allies, the Luhya, and members of other tribes in and Western Province.

One of those was his promise to give Kenyans a new constitution. But he refused to do so, although he had promised he would. when he campaigned across the country for constitutional changes.

Tribalism continued to be a major problem during his tenure. And his people, the economically and politically dominant Kikuyu, benefited the most.

The tragedy is compounded by the fact that national leaders themselves including presidents – from Jomo Kenyatta to Mwai Kibaki – have been some of the biggest offenders, practising tribalism, despite professions to the contrary and their public condemnation of the vice. And they know what tribalism does.

Divisive politics of ethnicity threaten national unity or the quest for it, especially in most African countries including Kenya where true national unity remains an elusive dream and is no more than a nebulous concept among the masses who can't see beyond their tribal borders and identities. Toxic politics of ethnicity tear not only the social fabric but the foundations of democratic institutions in young nations like Kenya where the people hardly have enjoyed any democracy. Ethnic politics also impede progress across the spectrum.

The 2007 electoral contest brought the matter into sharp focus probably as never before because of what it meant for the future of the country; a point underscored by many Kenyans and other people who knew what was going on. As Basette Bayuka, a news anchor for Kenya's independent National Television in Nairobi said in an interview with Voice of America (VOA) Africa News Service on 18 September 2007, tribalism would be a huge factor in the election in December. He was quoted in a

VOA Africa news report, "Kenya's Media Concerned About Tribal Sentiments in Politics," as saying:

Not so much of upset as concern about the general political landscape and the way it seems to be polarized along regional and ethnic groups.

Now, you look at Mwai Kibaki's Party of National Unity acronym PANU, and then you look at the pillars he's got around him. You got Musekari Kombo FORD-Kenya, perceived to be very strong in Western Province so expected to deliver that vote, and then you've got Uhuru Kenyatta, the leader of the official opposition, he is from the Kibaki's neck of the woods, Central Kenya. And he's thrown his weight behind the incumbent, and then you've got the retired President Daniel Arap Moi in that Rift Valley also, throwing his weight behind the incumbent.

So it's beginning to look like anyway the tribe factor would be key in this election. And indeed you can't rule out the ethnic factor, not in Kenyan politics, not in African politics.

He went on to say:

The interesting thing in Kenyan politics, you get these politicians and you ask them what is your party's platform, what ideology do you stand for that distinguishes ODM (Orange Democratic Movement) from ODM- Kenya (Orange Democratic Movement – Kenya) from PANU the Party for National Unity for instance. And you would find that it's more about personalities rather than real issues and ideologies.

As a result, it then comes down to the issue of where do you come from; Raila you come from Nyanza, Kalonzo you come from the Eastern Province, and then people looking what take is there in that for them....

It's all about trying to get as many votes as possible, and looking at those areas where you can tap into that and really its about ethnic calculations as well.

He also said that right from the beginning when Kenya adopted multi-party democracy in 1992, the first time the country had seriously tried to do so since independence, ethnicity and tribal sentiments had been key factors in the establishment of political parties:

Since Kenya went into multi-party democracy, that is way back in

182

1992, we had the first multi-party elections and KANU was still rather strong. But then a lot of the parties that sprung up thereafter, as time went along, started getting that tribal hue around them and they really became parties you could identify with a certain part of the country, as opposed to national parties.

Progressively, that is the way it's become. Tribalism is a real factor and we always keep challenging the politicians, how do you get rid of it?

I don't think anyone yet has gotten the antidote for that. It's going to be a factor, a real factor in this election.

And it's probably going to remain a factor for many years, not just in elections but in other areas of national life, keeping the country divided.

The chairman of Kenya's electoral commission, and the the chairman of the human rights commission in the country, expressed a collective sentiment about tribalism as a serious problem facing all Kenyans. According to a report by the Voice of America's Africa news service, "Kenyan Politics Marred by Tribalism, Says Human Rights Official," 27 September 2007:

> The chairman of Kenya's Human Rights Commission says the problem of tribalism and corruption in the country's body politic needs to be resolved.
>
> Maina Kiai said he agrees with the sentiments reportedly expressed by the chairman of the electoral commission that the politics in Kenya is marred by tribalism, violence and graft and that this year's election will be the true test of how far the country has come since single-party rule.
>
> It was reported last week that political tensions in Kenya have risen sharply this month. On Friday (21 September 2007), youths hurling rocks and firing arrows badly beat three of opposition presidential candidate Raila Odinga's top supporters when they arrived uninvited at a rural fundraiser organized by supporters of President Mwai Kibaki.
>
> From the capital, Nairobi, Maina Kiai tells reporter Peter Clottey that tribalism and corruption in Kenya's politics is no news.
>
> "These issues are not new, and indeed these sentiments are accurate. We have a serious problem of negative ethnicity in our society where political parties are organized on ethnic grounds and this has been our lot for the last 10 - 15 years. In addition, we have

endemic corruption that is from top to bottom and it makes a mockery of a lot of things that we have. We have a system of patronage where people want to get elected for patronage reasons, and they get support on that basis," Kiai explained.

He said Kenyans' hopes have been dashed by the Kibaki administration's lack of performance in the fight against corruption.

"We have been trying to change it; in fact we hoped that these past five years of this government would have made inroads into destroying this. But unfortunately, that would not be the case," he pointed out.

Kiai said President Kibaki abandoned his election promise to fight corruption.

"I think we must admit that the war against corruption by the government ended a couple of years ago.

I think they are making the right noises, but in terms of political action, you see a welcoming back of corruption; we have seen Daniel Arap Moi (former president) who has been accused in the Krol Report of being part of a conspiracy to take out of the country up to one billion pounds or two billion dollars and now completely supporting the Mwai Kibaki government.

You have seen no action taken on him; you have seen a number of reports that talk about endemic corruption simply being kept on the shelf.

So in a sense, I think you see this government has said goodbye to the war on corruption," Kiai pointed out.

He said he does not believe anyone of the current presidential aspirants has the antidote to cure the endemic nature of tribal sentiments across the country.

"Well you know the advantage that we have in Kenya is that we have many ethnic groups, and there is no really one dominant community. So what you are seeing then is these candidates coalescing around their ethnic groups, plus trying to get allies to them. And this, as I said, is not new.

If you look back at 2002, essentially, NARK under Mwai Kibaki, despite the promises of zero tolerance for corruption was basically ethnic-based, coming together against the Moi nominee. And I think you are seeing again the confirmation, and people going back and forth trying to figure out where they are on basically the same lines," he said.

Kiai was, however, hopeful the problem of tribalism in Kenya can be resolved.

"Absolutely, and it needs to be. And I think one of the first things we have to do is we begin moving from the constituency-based electoral politics to proportional representation, where people have lists that are national.

I think we need to see political leaders reaching out across the ethnic communities to bring people on board into high places of influence and responsibility.

We've got to see planning in terms of economic development to be much fairer so people would not have to get their own as president to have development," Kiai noted.

Tribalism had been a national phenomenon even during colonial rule when each tribe cared about itself and there wasn't much of what could be described as national loyalty to Kenya among the various ethnic groups.

But tribalism also acquired the stamp of legitimacy in national life when the first president of Kenya himself, Jomo Kenyatta, institutionalised the vice by favouring members of his own tribe, the Kikiyu, in all areas of national life. And no serious attempt has been to contain it, let alone to neutralise it.

In fact, one of the main reasons Kenyatta did not want Kenya to unite with Uganda and Tanganyika in 1963 was that he felt he would not be able to protect and promote the interests of his people, the Kikuyu, effectively in a larger political entity of an East African federation. Under his leadership, Kikuyu interests were paramount throughout Kenya.

But it would have been much harder for the Kikuyu to dominate the East African Federation even if Kenyatta became president of the macro-nation. As Tanzania's former president, Julius Nyerere, stated in one of his last interviews – not long before he died – with the *New Internationalist*, December 1998, although he did not explicitly say Jomo Kenyatta put the interests of the Kikuyu first, at the expense of those of other tribes:

I respected Jomo (Kenyatta) immensely. It has probably never happened before in history. Two heads of state, Milton Obote [Uganda's leader] and I, went to Jomo and said to him: 'Let's unite our countries and you be our head of state.' He said no.

I think he said no because it would have put him out of his

element as a Kikuyu Elder. - (Julius Nyerere, in the *New Internationalist*, December 1998, quoted by Godfrey Mwakikagile, *Nyerere and Africa: End of an Era*, New Africa Press, p. 145; and in Godfrey Mwakikagile, *Africa after Independence: Realities of Nationhood*, New Africa Press, p. 176).

Yet, Kenya prospered under Kenyatta's iron-fisted rule, relatively speaking, and would have done even much better had members of other tribes been given equal opportunity instead of being dominated by the Kikuyu and by the elite in general.

Kenya may still be "the star of the East" in the constellation of African nations, but it no longer shines as much as it used to.

And there may be hope from the younger generation if they pay attention to the old saying: A house divided can not stand.

It is also for the younger generation to stand up and demand fundamental change to make Kenya a better country for all.

Njonjo Mue addressed that subject in a speech to the annual conference of the Kenya Community Abroad (KCA) in St. Paul, Minnesota, in the United States in July 2000. The focus of the conference was on Kenya in the 21st century and Mue's speech was entitled, "Uhuru Generation: Taking a Stand on High Ground!":

The voice of our generation has been silent for far too long. Tonight, I want to speak to you about our role in Kenya's reconstruction and transformation as well as our vision for the country we wish to build and pass on to those who come behind us.

Not very long ago, Kenya was proudly referred to as the 'Shining Star of the East'. A rare African showcase.

It was a land where black and white lived together in peace; the economy was growing; the dignity of all was taken for granted, and we all knew a bit of what it was to be human -- to have food for our bodies, education for our minds, houses to live in and roads to travel on.

We shared what we had equitably, and where it was not enough to go round, we ensured that there was equal opportunity to compete for access to the riches of the land. We celebrated our strong but we also took care of our weak. For a while, the birthplace of humankind was also becoming the cradle of human hope.

But that was then.

To go to Kenya today is to descend into the valley of the shadow of death.

Our country is in darkness in more ways than one. Death strikes with unnerving frequency and ruthless efficiency - on our roads, in our hospitals, in ethnic clashes, through mob violence, even through bombs targeted at other people.

The walls we built to keep out the enemies of poverty, hunger and disease have all been torn down. God's children now huddle pitifully together, exposed to the elements of hopelessness, and vulnerable to the merciless chill of despair.

Today life in Kenya has become a meaningless search for meaning. Death is the only certainty we know – death of the body and spirit long before the death of the body. Kenya closely resembles Ezekiel's valley of dry bones. For we are surrounded by dry bones scattered over a patched and thirsty land.

They include massive corruption and looting of the resources of the land by their custodians, tribalism, collapsed systems, urban decay, rural underdevelopment, and so on.

We are all well aware of what ails our land, so I shall not dwell on it. Instead, allow me to focus on the two realities that we must confront.

Defining the Uhuru Generation:

I wish to remind you that throughout this discussion, I am an emissary of the Uhuru Generation. So I better take a moment and define who I am talking about.

The Uhuru Generation is the generation of women and men born after the midnight hour of 12 December 1963. They are the true daughters and sons of Kenya having been born in Kenya after the country joined the family of sovereign nations in contrast to those naturalized citizens like Daniel Arap Moi who had to give up the citizenship of Empire when Kenya was born in 1963.

Ours is the generation in whose name the struggle for independence was waged. But we now find ourselves impoverished and disinherited, aliens and sojourners in the land of our birth. We are the inheritors of an uneasy peace. But despite forming the overwhelming majority of Kenya's population today, we have largely been excluded from taking our full part in shaping the fortunes of our country.

Not only are we the majority of Kenya's masses, we also shoulder a disproportionate burden of Kenya's losses. Young people today bear the brunt of poverty, unemployment, HIV/AIDS, failed social services and collapsed infrastructure.

Not only has the political class stolen from us the tangible little luxuries of this life, they have deigned to take from us that which only the Creator can give and take by robbing us of the intangible qualities that define us as humans, – like hope, godly ambition, genuine peace of heart and mind, and the ability to dream of a better tomorrow.

We squint as we gaze at the horizon trying to make out the light of our new dawn but all we can see is darkness unending.

But it has not always been this dark. For across the sky of our long night of lost opportunities, there have been a few scattered stars. They have twinkled briefly to illuminate our collective path before flickering out again. We would not lament their demise had they not etched themselves on the edges of our consciousness.

The generation for which I speak is not ungrateful for the contributions of those gone before us. We are beholden to them.

In a word, we are not ungrateful to all the women, men and children who have given their lives in the search for peace and the struggle for human dignity in our homeland of Kenya. We celebrate their courage and their sacrifice.

But great though their accomplishments are, we must hasten to remind ourselves that a growing nation cannot afford to rest on its laurels, for its children will not find solace in its glorious past. We must confront present realities in order to march confidently into our common future.

We cannot continue to play second fiddle in the country that we own, while people who have clearly demonstrated that they have no stake in our future run it to the ground. Young people cannot sit by and let others define them or their mission on their own terms.

A country divided - Kenya's apartheid:

A country divided cannot stand. South Africa is a very good case study. I have heard a lot of people mistakenly saying that South Africa gained her independence in 1994. This is not true. South Africa gained independence in 1910. That was the year that the Union of South Africa was formed after the Anglo-Boer war resulted in the departure of the British colonialist.

But after the exit of the colonial rulers, a tiny minority of South Africa's population took the reigns of power and systematically oppressed the majority. This culminated in the introduction of formal apartheid rule in 1948 when the National Party government came to power. And as we all know majority rule was finally achieved in 1994 after a long and bloody struggle.

Kenya still yearns for her 1994

British colonists left in 1963, but we have not as yet achieved majority rule. Like South Africa, a minority group took the reigns of power after independence. The same group continues to oppress the majority to this day, with a few comings and goings.

The only difference is that unlike South Africa, the protagonists in Kenya are not defined by race. They are not even defined by tribe or class. They are defined by age and gender.

A tiny minority of old men led by Daniel Moi continues to ride roughshod over the majority of the people - mainly women and the Uhuru Generation.

But we should not merely point to the government, for it is by no means the only culprit. I am referring to the establishment as a whole. For just like apartheid in South Africa extended its tentacles to every facet of society, so too Kenya's minority of old males with one foot in the grave extends its rule everywhere, including the political Opposition, the institutions of learning, business, the church and the media.

And to merely ask Moi to leave office is equivalent to asking F. W. De Klerk to quit government while leaving the whole apartheid machine intact. Like Apartheid in South Africa, Kenya's Geriatric Oligarchy cannot be reformed. It must be dismantled.

That is why the message that must go out of St. Paul tonight, and reverberate in the ears of Mr. Moi and Mr. Kibaki; Mr. Nyachae and Mr. Saitoti; Mr. Muite and Mr. Raila, is as simple as it is profound. GENTLEMEN, END THIS APARTHEID NOW!

But for those who might find the apartheid paradigm uncomfortable, let me approach the same conclusion from another direction. When a monarch dies leaving an heir who is too young to rule, a Regent is appointed to oversee the affairs of state until the heir becomes of age.

Well, I submit to you that the time has come for the regents appointed on our behalf in 1963 to get out of the way, for the rightful heirs to Kenya's throne have finally come of age.

Throwing old men into the sea?

But, one might ask, what about our tradition and the place it accords to elders? Are we throwing all that away?

189

The answer is no. We are not advocating that we throw all old men into the sea (though their performance lately has caused the thought to cross our minds). We will continue to value their wisdom and their experience.

We are not departing from tradition, but enforcing it.

For Africans never did send their old and their frail into the battlefield. We listened keenly to their whispers of wisdom. But it is the young that must go to the front line and face the enemy.

What enemies do we face today?

We face the challenges of the information revolution - what sense does it make to send someone who has never used a computer to the frontline?

We face the challenge of globalization - What sense does it make to promote somebody to the rank of General by virtue only of the fact that he studied economics at the LSE in the early sixties?

We face extinction through HIV and AIDS - what sense does it make to let a conservative old man who cannot mention the word 'sex' without biting his tongue command our troops?

We face humiliation as a people and indignity as a race - What sense does it make to prop up Lieutenants by virtue only of the fact that their colour is acceptable to those to whom we extend our begging bowls?

Not only does it not make sense to recruit from among the ranks of the old and infirm, we should also be careful to recruit soldiers with demonstrated loyalty to our cause. For we have been jilted for far too long and cheated far too often. We have had our hearts broken when we found suitors who had vowed to remain forever faithful to our cause in bed with those ravishing us.

But even though we are a hurting people today, I must state emphatically that we are not a desperate people; what's more, we much wiser for our experiences. Consequently, we shall no longer take our latter day saints at their word. You cannot sup with the devil one day and then anoint yourself our savior the next.

And so even as we nurse our wounds, we need to marshal supreme confidence and demonstrate to the world that Kenyans and Africans are not the children of a lesser god. We cannot do so without the wisdom and experience of the elders, but they must not purport to fight the battles of our time for us.

That, we must do for ourselves.

Without a vision

I suppose by now you are all thinking that I am being a bit tough on the old folk and blaming them for everything. Well, not quite. The last dry bone in Kenya's wasteland of lost opportunities is one for which we all share a responsibility. It is the bone of a lack of a vision.

To what does our government aspire beyond perpetuating its own stay in power? What does the opposition work for beyond trying to capture that power? What are we as a people working for beyond mere survival?

In short what is the vision for our country?

In the history of our nationhood, we have often substituted platitudes for vision. In the 1970's and 80's the government promised that there would be electricity for all by the year 2000; water for all by the year 2000; education for all by the year 2000; health for all by the year 2000.

Well, 2000 is halfway gone and on all scores we are worse off than we were when these empty promises were made. Like all the empty promises of yesteryear, the latest round, including that of industrialization by 2020, are just hollow platitudes.

One is tempted to think that at the time of these extravagant promises, the Kenyan government seems to have hoped that the world would end by the year 2000 - in which case all their promises would be fulfilled in heaven. Now that the end is not nigh, one wonders what next, mass suicide? Well, not quite. But perhaps the equivalent seeing as the government is doing all it can to encourage Kenyans to immigrate abroad where at least there is electricity, water and education for all in the year 2000.

But it behooves our generation to define a new vision for our country and to draw a road-map to a new dispensation. We cannot wait for the government to do this for us. We must somehow find the courage to forge a new consensus for the country that we wish to build and bequeath to those who come behind us. We might be able to draw some inspiration from our past achievements, few though they are, but we cannot hope to find the answer for our tomorrows in our yesterdays.

But why is vision important?

There are two main reasons.

First, 'without a vision the people perish'. The word for 'perish' in the original Hebrew does not actually mean physical death. It means that people go naked and are impoverished. But one does not need to understand Hebrew to see that this is exactly the state we are in today. We can blame our woes on any number of people - Parliament blames Biwott, for the power rationing; Biwott blames Kibaki and Nyachae; Nyachae says Moi should take responsibility; Moi says he was not a rainmaker!

191

Every time a catastrophe strikes us. We can round up all the usual suspects - Moi, Kenyatta, constitutional reform, colonial rule, world economic order, the weather, my neighbour's tribe, your sister's gender, and so on.

But I came all the way from Johannesburg to St. Paul today, to let you know that we are doomed to go round in circles - to repeat the same mistakes, to play the blame game, to wallow in the valley of despair - until we apprehend the real culprit: Our own loss of a dream; our own lack of vision.

The second reason why vision is vital is this:

Without a future, human beings are programmed to go back to their past.

Every time the children of Israel lost sight of the Promised Land they demanded of Moses that he take them back to Egypt. A man who sees no future in his marriage will return to his multiple partners. And ask any police investigator where they go to look for a convict who has escaped from jail - they go to all the places where he used to hang out.

Tragically, we see many examples of that in Kenya today. Children are doing homework by candlelight tonight, families eat in darkness in scenes reminiscent of the 1960s. We have also taken to appointing white Kenyans to important positions, not necessarily because they are competent, but in a cynical attempt to win favour from our former colonizers who instinctively trust their own kind more than they trust us.

Even more tragically, I have heard intelligent people ask, "If only the British would come back and colonize us!"

Without a future, we have gone back to our past. Without a vision, the people are perishing.

But we must never give up hope. It is not too late to define a new vision for our country. This is the vision of the Uhuru Generation:

We shall build a strong, united and prosperous African country comprising a diverse multicultural society, with a vibrant economy providing equal opportunity for individual and communal growth; and where freedom, human dignity and respect for the rights of all will be the basis of social behaviour by the citizen and the State alike.

But what will separate our vision from the 'by the year 2000' platitudes I spoke about earlier?

By constantly remembering that vision without action is fiction; by developing programmes that are carefully design to make our vision a reality, and by moving beyond merely talking about our problems to actually individually owning them and mobilizing our own physical and intellectual resources to reclaim out land of promise.

And of vital importance, we must remember that we will never attain our vision in the sense that we can sit down and rest. We must forever keep it ahead of us so that it can define our purpose, set our boundaries and parameters and test our character, individually and collectively.

And when the Uhuru Generation itself becomes older, and if we have been faithful in staying on the path, we shall not fear to hand over to the next generation to continue to build upon the promise.

Epilogue:

I wish to end where I began, with the Prophet Ezekiel at the valley of the dry bones:

"Young woman, young man, can these bones live again?"

The answer lies in the eye of the Beholder
For if we focus only
On the legacy bequeathed us
By those gone before us
A legacy of wasted years and lost days
Of greed and corruption, vice and violence
Of shattered lives and broken dreams
Then we can only but see dry bones
At the bottom of the desolate valley
Of our painful yesterdays.

But if we lift up our eyes unto the hills
And focus our gaze
On the distant horizons
Of our new tomorrows
If we defy the odds and rebuild together
If we make God our closest ally
And vision our guiding principle

Then we shall see our homeland of Kenya
Once again becoming A heritage of splendour.

Like the members of any other generation, the younger people of the Uhuru generation born after 12 December 1963 when Kenya won independence hope that they will leave this world a better place than they found it. And if they do, they will make Kenya a better place for everybody.

193

It will be a country where people will be judged by their intrinsic worth as individuals - regardless of who and what they are - and as fellow countrymen, and not on the basis of where they come from or what tribe or race they belong to.

Unfortunately, that remains only a dream, and a distant goal, in this magnificent land of enormous potential.

Chapter Nine:

Kenya's National Character

LIKE most African countries, Kenya is plagued by tribalism. It is a nation fractured along ethno-regional lines.

Yet it exists as a single political entity whose identity has been forged on the anvil of diversity. And it is identified by certain attributes which collectively constitute what can be called its national character.

The concept of national character is nebulous, and highly controversial, especially in young nations like those of Africa which are often dismissed as no more than a hodge-podge of different and antagonistic ethnic groups lumped together with very little in common in terms of identity except their "African-ness" as a people who share the same continent.

Yet, it is a concept that exists in reality and can be demonstrated by empirical evidence. And it has been given concrete expression in the establishment of nations which assume their own distinctive identities, hence national characters, as they evolve through the years.

In the case of old nations, it has taken centuries for them to solidify their identities and national characters.

Still, all nations have their own characteristics shaped by their beliefs and values including moral values, traditions and customs, learnt and taught - individually and collectively - from childhood through adulthood from generation to generation.

Sometimes, inculcation of those beliefs, ideals and values takes the form of indoctrination. And they shape individual characters and collective attitudes which are an integral part of national character.

The concept of national character has even been attributed to a grand design by the Divine. For example, German nationalist philosopher Johann Fichte defined a nation as a manifestation of divine order.

In his *Addresses to The German Nation* he delivered as lectures at the University of Berlin, he contended that the German people existed as a natural collective entity constituting an indivisible organic whole and spoke a language, the German language, which had naturally evolved and been structured to express the truth.

And since Germany did not have natural frontiers (mountains or large rivers or an ocean around its borders), like her neighbour France, for example, did; he argued that the German language itself formed inner frontiers – uniting the German people while keeping foreigners out – and thus constituted natural boundaries for the German nation. Tanzanians and Kenyans can probably say the same thing about Kiswahili!

Nations can indeed exist without land and physical boundaries. The case of the Palestinians is a typical example in contemporary times. They don't have a country as a sovereign political entity yet they do exist as a nation. Before then it was the Jews until the establishment of Israel as a political entity in 1948 at the expense of the Palestinian Arabs.

Fichte's concept of the nation as a manifestation of divine order, combined with his fanatical patriotism, stimulated German nationalism.

Among Italian nationalists like Mazzini and Garibaldi who sought the unification of Italy, Italy's natural (physical) frontiers defined the Italian nation as a natural entity inhabited by Italians with their own national character. Mazzini even invoked the shape of Italy - with its physical barriers as borders - to argue that it was meant to define the Italian nation with its own distinctive identity and characteristics different from those of other nations.

Italian nationalists also argued that God had intended for them, as Italians or as an Italian nation, to occupy that land The implication was obvious. The land was intended exclusively for them as Italians with their own distinctive identity and attributes as a people.

And in many fundamental respects, especially in terms of inner frontiers, not necessarily with regard to national language as defined by Fichte but mostly in terms of their own characteristics including collective attitudes and values which distinguish them, African nations are no exception as entities with their own unique characters.

For example, it is common to hear quite often people talk about Nigerians, what kind of people they are. Among their best attributes is that they are very ambitious and are high achievers. And there are quite a few bad things said about them, of course, just like any other people.

Ghanaians also have their own characteristics. Under Nkrumah, they were able to achieve a degree of unity, as one people, unheard of in most African countries because of Nkrumah's ability to fight tribalism and regionalism. And he instilled in his people a sense of national pride in a way most African leaders did not or were not able to, besides Nyerere and very few others.

Even today, many Ghanaians identify themselves first as Ghanaians, not as Ewe, Fanti, Ga, or Dagomba; while it's not uncommon to hear Nigerians say, "I'm Yoruba," or "I'm Igbo," before they say "I'm Nigerian"; or Kenyans say "I'm Kikuyu, Kamba, Luo, or Luhya" before they say, "I'm Kenyan."

Also many Ghanaians are some of the most Pan-Africanist-oriented people because of what Nkrumah taught and the role Ghana – under his leadership – played in supporting the African liberation movements the way Tanzania did under Nyerere.

It is an enduring legacy, left by Nkrumah, which has played a critical role in shaping Ghana's identity and national character.

All those are attributes or characteristics of national character - whether Ghana's, Kenya's or Nigeria's or of any other country.

While it is true that African countries don't have solid national identities like the old nations of Europe and Asia whose identities have been forged through the centuries and have had the benefit of time - many centuries - to take shape, there is no question that they have individual attributes which distinguish them from each other in a number of ways; although they also have a lot in common as fellow Africans and as young nations or political entities which attained sovereign status only a few decades ago, mostly in the sixties.

One of the fundamental differences between European nations and African nations is that the establishment of nations in Europe preceded the creation of states – institutions of authority over given territory – while in Africa, the reverse was the case.

States preceded the establishment of nations – they were established even before countries were formed and before the people developed a sense of loyalty to the country they shared as "one people."

In Africa, states as instruments of authority were created by the colonial powers to bring different tribes together into a cohesive whole, the countries we have today, to facilitate colonial administration. And there is a lot that still has to be done to weld these ethnic groups together into truly cohesive entities transcending ethnic and regional loyalties and be able to establish truly united nations.

But even in their infancy, as entities which have existed as independent nation-states only for the past 40 years or so since the end of colonial rule, they do have their own identities. And these identities have largely been shaped by the political leadership which assumed power on attainment of sovereign status in the sixties and in a few cases (like Ghana and Guinea) in the late fifties.

Thus, you had Jomo Kenyatta, The Burning Spear, whose formidable personality had such a profound impact on the development and evolution of the modern state, hence nation, of what we know as Kenya today that it is virtually impossible to think or talk about Kenya without also at least thinking about Kenyatta at the same time. He ruled with an iron fist, shaped his country in his image, and preferred continuity rather than change.

He left almost everything virtually intact after the British officially relinquished power on independence day, 12 December 1963, as if nothing had changed.

Preservation or continuation of the status quo, the way the British ran the country, played a critical role in shaping Kenya's national character to the point where even today, it is not unusual to hear some Africans from other countries say, "Kenyans are very British," they "worship" the British, or that they are "subservient" to the white man. And the country remained solidly capitalist after independence.

Stereotypes sometimes correspond to reality, and not all characterisations are stereotypes. Perceptions of Kenyans – and other Africans - as to what type of people they are sometimes reflect reality.

But it does not mean that Kenyans are really subservient to the white man or are "very British"; what it really means is that many Kenyans admire British achievements in many areas especially in terms of education and material civilisation, although there are some people – not just in Kenya but in other African countries as well, including my home country Tanzania –

who think that they are "civilised" if they copy the manners of their former colonial masters - British or French - or "act white" and even sound British or French; and ape the consumption proclivities of their former imperial masters whom they see as the paragon of virtue and the embodiment of what is best in mankind.

That is colonial mentality at its worst. And it is typical of many Africans, especially among the elite, who not only admire and even "worship" our former colonial masters; they are mesmerised by the glitter and glamour of the West, the same place our conquerors came from, and whose nations continue to exploit us.

Even today, there are many Africans who try to be carbon copies of our former colonial masters and are more "British," and more "French," than the British and the French themselves.

The same people who conquered us and who continue to exploit us are glorified by some of us as our heroes as if we don't have our own heroes, and as if we never even had any before the coming of Europeans. Glorifying our conquerors as our heroes is the worst form of colonial mentality and mental slavery.

The British are among those who are glorified by a significant number of Kenyans and other Africans who were once ruled by them.

This kind of admiration and glorification also fuels imperial arrogance, best exemplified by an old English lady who once asked Tom Mboya on a street in London: "Which one of our possessions are you from?"

These are the kind of people who already have an inflated ego. So glorifying them, and admiring them so much, only makes things worse.

There is no question that British influence is still very strong in Kenya even today more than 40 years after independence. And all the governments which have been in power in all those years have chosen to maintain the status quo instead of opting for fundamental change across

200

the spectrum in the way the country is run and how the country's wealth is shared.

It is clear that the British played a major role in shaping Kenya's national character.

It could even be argued that the people of Kenya and Tanganyika differed in national character even before independence; with Kenya's national character having been partly, if not largely, shaped by the British settlers who settled in Kenya in very large numbers during colonial rule.

They were highly visible, they spread their values - directly and indirectly - and were seen by many Kenyans, not just by the elite, as role models to be emulated. And there are still many whites of British descent still living in Kenya today. Many of them are citizens, others are not and have no interest in becoming citizens.

Tanganyika, on the other hand, had far fewer settlers than Kenya did. There were about 66,000 settlers, mostly British, in Kenya during the fifties not long before the country won independence. Tanganyika had between 21,000 and 23,000, also mostly British.

If the former British rulers were to return to Kenya today, they would notice very little change in the way the country is run in terms of institutional arrangements, attitudes, values and even moral traits which are some of the characteristics which collectively constitute national character. They would also notice that many Kenyans, black Kenyans, are indeed "very British."

It has been an entirely different story in neighbouring Tanzania where Julius Nyerere, a charismatic personality, dominated the political scene for almost 40 years from independence in 1961 until his death in 1999.

He sought fundamental change in his quest for socialist transformation of Tanzania in order to build an egalitarian society and successfully welded almost 130 different ethnic groups and racial minorities into a solidly united and peaceful nation unparalleled in the history of post-colonial Africa, giving Tanzania and Tanzanians a unique national character.

The egalitarian ideals he instilled in the people of Tanzania played a critical role in shaping their national character.

They not only transcended tribalism under his leadership; they also came to accept each other as equals in terms of rights and dignity as fellow Tanzanians and as fellow human beings in a society where no one was better than another simply because he or she was rich or belonged to a certain tribe.

In Kenya the entrepreneurial spirit under capitalism went long ways in shaping Kenya's national character. Kenyans are said to be more "aggressive," more "enterprising," and more "daring" than Tanzanians.

By remarkable contrast, Tanzanians, shaped by the egalitarian ideals of ujamaa (familyhood) and compassion and respect for fellow man taught by Nyerere, are known to be "humble," "more reserved," "trustworthy," "more patient," "compassionate," and "non-tribalistic" unlike their Kenyan neighbours who have a reputation for being very tribalistic, "very individualistic" and "selfish."

And the fact that tribalism was institutionalised under Kenyatta has meant that this vice – or virtue depending on who the beneficiary is – has played a critical role in shaping Kenya's national character distinctly different from Tanzania's.

In Kenya tribalism is accepted as a way of life, a way of doing things or of getting things done.

Therefore, tribalism has not only shaped Kenya's national character; among many Kenyans – not all but many – tribalism is celebrated as a virtue and is not seen as a vice to be despised. It is not only a way of getting ahead in life; it is also a means to promote and protect the interests of "my people," that is, of "my fellow tribesmen," at the expense of other Kenyans, of course.

So, Kenya exists as nation, yes. But it is a nation that is

divided from within, fractured along ethnic and regional lines.

Yet its weakness, tribalism, is one of the most prominent attributes of its national character. Many Kenyans say "We are one nation, but my tribe comes first." Otherwise it is not the Kenya we know if we contend otherwise.

That is in sharp contrast to what goes on in Tanzania where tribalism is not a major problem. It has not been eradicated but it has been effectively contained, and has even been virtually neutralised in many areas of national life.

To most people in Tanzania, tribalism is not a virtue, it is a vice. It is not glorified; it is despised. It is not something to be proud of.

Even speaking one's tribal language in front of members of other tribes is frowned upon in Tanzania. That is not the case in Kenya.

All that is part of Tanzania's national character. Most Tanzanians see themselves as Tanzanians first; not as Digo, Nyamwezi, Nyakyusa, Zigua, Zaramo, Chaga, Ngoni, Yao, Makua, Sukuma, Luguru, Hehe, Ndengereko, Fipa, Safwa, Gogo, Bena, Bondei, Haya, Sambaa, Nyika, Luguru or Makonde among many other tribes.

But while Tanzanians have transcended tribalism, the question that now arises in this era of globalisation after the triumph of capitalism over communism and socialism is whether or not the entrepreneurial spirit that has taken hold in Tanzania, after the country renounced socialism as a state ideology, will also re-mould Tanzania's national character and transform the country into a place where the people no longer care about each other and no longer see each other as one and as equal human beings as in neighbouring Kenya.

In Kenya, the entrepreneurial spirit under which the country has thrived since independence as a capitalist society has remarkably shaped Kenya's national character and has radically transformed the country into a nation characterised by ruthless competition.

The emphasis is on competition, not on cooperation or compassion, because raw-naked individualism is celebrated as a virtue. It is a product of capitalism and the acquisitive instinct nurtured in a society which is itself a product of western material civilisation.

In Tanzania, this highly competitive spirit is not very pronounced even today among the vast majority of the people - at least not as much as it is in Kenya - and was virtually non-existent under socialism; although there is a lot of competition nowadays among the elite and the urban dwellers in general in terms of employment and earning income by various means including self-employment especially in the subterranean economy.

During the socialist era especially in the early seventies when there was so much rhetoric about the virtues of socialism versus capitalism, it was not uncommon to hear some Tanzanians saying, "Kenya is a dog-eat-dog society"; to which Kenyans responded by saying, "In Tanzania, it's dog eating nothing!"; a statement that was given prominence when it was also made by the arrogant Kenyan attorney general, Charles Njonjo, in 1977.

It was common knowledge among the Kenyan elite that Tanzanian President Julius Nyerere did not like Charles Njonjo and had no respect for him because he saw him as arrogant and callous towards the plight of the poor, as he did other members of the Kenyan elite, of course; an observation also made by Kenyan Professor Ali Mazrui in his moving eulogy - "Nyerere and I" - when Nyerere died in October 1999. As he stated in his memorial tribute to Nyerere:

With his concept of Ujamaa, Nyerere also attempted to build bridges between indigenous African thought and modern political ideas. Ujamaa, which means "familyhood", was turned by Nyerere into a foundation for African Socialism. Ujamaa became the organising principle of the entire economic experiment in Tanzania from the Arusha Declaration of 1967 to the mid-1980s.

His relations with the Kenyan political elite deteriorated further and further. He found Attorney-General Charles Njonjo particularly distasteful and arrogant as a person and reckless in his attitudes towards Kenya's neighbours. Nyerere was fond of Mzee Kenyatta, but he thought Njonjo exercised disproportionate influence on the old man. Nyerere was not sure whether to be amused or outraged when Njonjo turned any discussion on Kenyatta's mortality into something close to a capital offence!

Nyerere was against turning rulers into gods - "Like the old Pharaohs of ancient Egypt." Making Kenyatta immortal was like turning him into a god.

Nyerere and I remembered the proposal which was made in 1964 to celebrate annually the day of Kenyatta's arrest by the British as "the Last Supper". There was such a strong negative reaction from Christian churches in Kenya against using the concept of "the Last Supper" in this way that the idea was dropped....

Tanzania was one of the few African countries which attempted to find its own route to development instead of borrowing the ideologies of the West....

Nyerere's policies of nation-building amount to a case of Unsung Heroism. With wise and strong leadership, and with brilliant policies of cultural integration, he took one of the poorest countries in the world and made it a proud leader in African affairs and an active member of the global community....

In global terms, he was one of the giants of the 20th Century....He did bestride this narrow world like an African colossus....

Julius Nyerere was my Mwalimu too. It was a privilege to learn so much from so great a man. - (Ali A. Mazrui, "Nyerere and I," at Africa Resource Center: africaresource.com/content/view/56/222).

While Nyerere's socialist policies did not succeed in developing Tanzania and did not transform the country into a truly socialist society, the idealism which inspired those policies united the people of Tanzania in their quest for equality across the spectrum in a way they probably would not have been able to pursue the same goal under capitalism.

That was in sharp contrast to what happened in neighbouring Kenya where equality meant nothing. And it still means nothing even today.

And when Kenyan Attorney-General Charles Njonjo ridiculed Tanzania as a "dog eating nothing" society – not only because of the failure of socialism but also because it was a society of egalitarian ideals where the people shared poverty and whatever "little" they had as a country, instead of encouraging individuals to accumulate personal wealth at the expense of others – he epitomized Kenya's national character and one of its best or worst attributes: selfishness.

And it is an attribute that still defines Kenya today. It is an integral part of Kenya's national character and psyche in a country where ruthless competition is glorified as a virtue and where tribalism - which is itself a form of competition and selfishness - is the very essence of national life and one's well-being.

It does not mean that Kenyans in general are selfish; nor does it mean that there are no selfish people in Tanzania – there are plenty, especially among the elite and even among ordinary people.

What it means is that Kenyans, after living under capitalism for decades since independence, are animated by a spirit of individualism and entrepreneurship in a way their brethren in Tanzania are not. That is because this kind of spirit was stifled by socialism among the vast majority of the people in Tanzania.

You can not thrive under capitalism without being highly competitive. In fact, capitalism is ruthless - and even heartless - by nature. Each to his own.

But it is also highly productive and provides the best incentives to production. Yet it fosters inequality.

In Tanzania, socialism not only stifled individual initiative; it also sometimes compromised standards of excellence which are encouraged under capitalism.

But socialism also had its virtues: the egalitarian ideals which fostered national unity and equality among Tanzanians its antithesis, capitalism, did not in Kenya.

Even today collective consciousness, an attribute

206

Tanzanians share, is rare among Kenyans except in a tribal context.

Loyalty to the tribe takes precedence over loyalty to the nation among most Kenyans.

Individualism and tribalism are deeply embedded in the national psyche. And it is impossible to understand Kenya's national character without comprehending or coming to grips with this harsh reality.

If the existence of nations is indeed a manifestation of divine order, there is an imperative need for all nations to improve and for some even to change their national characters. Kenya is no exception.

And if Kenya decides to do that, the ideals of justice, equality, fairness, compassion and concern for the well-being of others which inspired the struggle for independence and led to the birth of a new nation may one day become some of the finest qualities, and some of the most outstanding attributes, of her national character transmitted from one generation to the next.

Appendix I:

Race and Culture:
A Luo Perspective

PHILIP OCHIENG' is a veteran journalist and political analyst at the *Daily Nation*, Nairobi, Kenya, where he is also one of the editors.

He once worked at the *Daily News,* Dar es Salaam, Tanzania, in the early seventies as a columnist.

One of the people he worked with at the *Daily News* was Godfrey Mwakikagile, a news reporter, later an author, whose book *Ethnic Politics in Kenya and Nigeria*, a comparative study, proved indispensable in the completion of this work, especially the chapter on ethnic conflicts in Kenya in the nineties.

Philip Ochieng' is a member of the Luo ethnic group, one of the largest in Kenya and in the entire East Africa whose home region is Nyanza Province on the shores of Lake Victoria in the western part of the country, and he had the following to say about some cultural aspects of the Luo way of life in this commentary in *The East African*, a weekly and sister publication of the *Daily Nation*:

From Home Squared to the US Senate:
How Barack Obama Was Lost and Found

The East African, Nairobi, Kenya
Monday, 1 November 2004

When Barack Obama Junior first visited "Home Squared" – Barack Senior's native village in Alego in the early 1990s – they confronted him with the perplexing accusation: "You're lost!" The words are English. Yet Barack Junior had never heard them in that context. For the idea they express is totally Luo.

It is a literal translation of the phrase *ilal* – from the intransitive verb *lal*, to disappear or to be away for a long time without an explanation, and the transitive verb *lalo*, to lose something. In Chicago's South Side, Barack Junior's adopted home, they have a homely way of expressing *ilal*: "Long time no see!"

But *lal* has a number of figurative meanings – to lose a line of thought, to deviate from the norm, to discard tradition. Simply by being born and growing up in America, Barack Junior had never been a Luo: He had *lal*.

And yet – because ours is a fiercely patriarchal community – Barack Junior is a Luo by the sheer fact that Barack Senior was a Luo. Barack Junior was thus doubly "lost." For, in important of ways, Barack Senior himself had for a long time "lost the way."

First, through classroom tutelage, he had imbibed the white man's culture. It was in this sense that Abong'o (as Roy now prefers to be known) and Auma – Barack Senior's children by his original (Luo) wife – had also "gone astray."

Educated in Germany and now a University of Nairobi

209

lecturer, Auma was living in a relatively comfortable suburban home in Nairobi when Barack Junior came to Kenya. It was for this reason that she considered her Alego home to be "Home Squared. As we learned in the S.M. Otieno case, the Luo elite consider their urban residences to be mere "houses."

Their real homes are in the countryside, where they or their parents were born. Which is why whenever one takes a vacation, one pronounces with great pride: "*Adhi dala!*" – "I am going home!" Auma preferred to give the two places equal significance. To which Abong'o quipped that, in that case, for Barack Obama Junior, Alego was "Home Cubed."

Finally, Barack Senior had lost his way by marrying a white woman – Barack Junior's mother. This is the fate that he shares with James McBride, the black American autobiographer.

McBride's book, *The Colour of Water,* is subtitled *A Black Man's Tribute to His White Mother*. Barack Obama Junior's book is titled *Dreams from My Father*. If he had inserted the word "black" in the title, the parallel would have been more striking.

But, even inside the covers, the community of themes is stark. No matter where he is, a black person always lives in two worlds. Obama Junior shares with my daughter Juliette Akinyi the fact that they are Americans with Kenyan fathers whom they never really knew.

Obama Senior left Anne – Junior's mother – almost as soon as Junior was born. Junior met Senior only once. When he was 12, Senior visited him in Honolulu, Hawaii, where Junior was growing up under the care of his white grandfather and grandmother. They never saw each other again.

Because I recognise myself in it, this is the most moving theme in Barack Obama's book – the scar that this fact left in Junior's mind, the enduring crisis of identity that will not go away.

Like Obama Senior, I too went to the US on the famous Tom Mboya Airlift of 1959 [when hundreds of Kenyan students were given scholarships to American universities]. I first met Obama Senior in Tom Mboya's Nairobi office [Mboya was then the secretary general of the Kenya Federation of Labour]. Obama and I met up again on returning to Nairobi and remained drinking buddies for many years.

Back in the US, Nova Diane and I had left each other as soon as Akinyi was born in Chicago. Akinyi is now in her early 40s and yet we have never seen each other. We never even communicated until three years ago, when she finally traced me by e-mail.

Barack Obama Junior's book only serves to remind me of the agony that has oppressed Akinyi's mind all these years. The only consolation, if it is one, is that all black people – no matter where they are – really live in two worlds and, therefore, have an identity crisis.

One might even say that they live in no world. Even in our native Africa, *walal* ("we are lost"). When, by agency of Christian missionaries, European imperialism drove our forefathers' communal spirit away from the land, we stopped being African. We started trying to think like Europeans. But we never became Europeans either. We became ghosts flitting into and out of European imagination.

Our own Ngugi wa Thiong'o has been telling us for decades – what we have refused to hear – that as long as we continue to worship European gods, European ideas on governance and European paradigms of development, all our endowments – labour, natural resources and markets – will continue to belong to Europe for the fleecing.

By seeking to enter white America's centre of power, Barack Obama Junior, who is almost certain to become a US Senator in this week's elections, may himself be accused of surrender to a "democracy" that is in essence an "elective tyranny," the white liberal's political prescription

211

for perpetuating an economic-intellectual system that dehumanises the black person.

But we must also reject simplistic solutions, such as the all-or-nothingism that posits – like Ngugi's own position on the English language – that nothing at all can be gained through the institutions of the oppressor. There is much that a would-be liberator can glean from the inside.

Barack Obama Junior's grassroots activities among the oppressed of Chicago's South Side show that he is keenly aware of his people's suffering and needs. They prove that he has not gone over to the white man's world.

Mention in his book of certain Chicago locations – like Cottage Grove, 95th Street, Hyde Park, Michigan Avenue, Buckingham Fountain, the Lakeside Drive, the Gold Coast – rekindle fond memories of when I was an undergraduate in the Loop. Having spent four formative years in the "Windy City", I easily identify myself with them and with him.

I know that, elected to the Senate, he will not forget his people in Hawaii and Home Squared. Indeed, throughout the black world. Nay, throughout the whole world because – as Mwalimu Julius Nyerere used to say – all oppressed people of all colours *ni Waswahili*.

This was perhaps why marrying a white woman didn't bother Barack Senior. And there is much to be said for that woman's own mental and moral courage that she was willing to join a black man whose world was as far away as the moon and in a country where such a marriage could prove opprobrious.

There was, however, another white woman. That was why, when I first heard of Obama Junior, I assumed that he was Ruth's son. Ruth was the wife I knew after Obama Senior came back from America and worked for Tom Mboya in the Ministry of Economic Planning.

After Obama Senior had left Anne in Honolulu, he studied at Harvard, where he met and befriended Ruth. She afterwards followed him all the way to Home

212

Squared. I assumed that Junior was either David or Mark, Ruth's two sons whose names I no longer remembered.

What I remember, however – and much of it emerges from Obama Junior's book – was that Obama Senior's marriage to Ruth was not a happy one. Like his father, although charming, generous and extraordinarily clever, Obama Senior was also imperious, cruel and given to boasting about his brain and his wealth.

It was this kind of boasting that proved his undoing in the Kenyatta system – although, as he said, there was tribalism in it –and left him without a job, plunged him into prolonged poverty and dangerously wounded his ego.

Like me, he was excessively fond of Scotch. In his later years, he had fallen into the habit of going home drunk every night. This was what forced Ruth to sue for a divorce to marry another friend of mine, a Tanzanian.

Scotch, indeed, was what proved to be Obama Senior's final undoing. Driving a car always excited him excessively.

Obama Senior had had many extremely serious accidents. In time, both his legs had to be amputated and replaced with iron. But his pride was such that he could not tolerate "crawling like an insect" on the road. I was not surprised when I learned how he had finally died.

I was more surprised when Obama Junior emerged, as if from the blue. I knew that Home Squared, Luoland, Kenya and Africa might soon be represented in the world's most powerful council.

In this way, Barack Obama Junior was not lost.

Appendix II:

Indians of East Africa

Rudy Brueggemann

First written in 1997 and updated in May 2000

I met Shabir on a packed 747 jet, flying from Dar es Salaam, Tanzania, to London. A Tanzanian national and Shiite Moslem, the 40-year-old ethnic Indian businessman now calls Houston, Texas, his home.

Despite this transglobal lifestyle across two hemispheres, Shabir was every bit the East African Indian that he was born. Family and business formed Shabir's founding bedrocks, as they did for thousands of East African Indians claiming dual lives in England, Canada, and the United States.

Shabir said he still runs a mercantile store in Dar es Salaam with his nephews, even though he makes more money as a laborer in the United States, where he has lived for seven years and now holds a green card.

Shabir's U.S. employer, a glass-making plant, pays him $10 an hour plus time and a half for overtime, he said proudly. He sweeps floors and does odd jobs at the facility.

His brothers and sisters fare even better in South Carolina and Los Angeles, running glass shops themselves. But, a businessman at heart, he enjoys yearly visits to his mother country to check up on his family business.

A nervous, short man with glasses, Shabir complained repeatedly about American divorce law once he learned I was American. "The man loses everything. This is no good," he told me, voicing a conservative African and Indian custom placing the man in charge of the all-important economic unit - the family.

Shabir, however, did not complain about his new-found prosperity. He would become a U.S. citizen when he returned to the United States because he loved America. He loved the opportunity to make money and to escape persecution, which ethnic Indian Tanzanians had experienced in the late 1960s when many left the then-socialist country. Still, he said, he would retain his family/business ties in Africa.

On this newly started Alliance Airlines flight to London, three of four passengers could trace ancestors from modern-day India and Pakistan - Sikhs, Moslems, Hindus alike. But today, they resided in East Africa, as well as England and North America.

Indians from Uganda living in Canada. Indians from Kenya living in London. Indians born in Tanzania and living in the United States.

Shabir was one of the many Indians I encountered at every point on my East African trip.

The security guard at the Vancouver, Canada, airport who checked my hand luggage claimed Uganda as his familial home. My safari company in Arusha, Tanzania, called Roy Safaris, was run by a Goan Indian family. The woman travel agent for Alliance Airline's Dar es Salaam office was a Hindu Indian.

The owners of my hotel in Zanzibar's Old Stone city

were Moslem Indian. My money changer in Kigali, Rwanda, still another ethnic Indian. Even one of my bus drivers in rural northeast Uganda, a short, bearded man - cocky enough to yell in Swahili at a truck filled with beer-guzzling Ugandan soldiers - was Indian.

Though Indians pervade every facet of East African commercial life, their presence in this region remains far less known in America compared to the much romanticized - and fictionalized - legacy of the East Africa's white settlers who imported the Indians as coolie laborers in the late 1800s to build the Uganda-Kenya railway.

Of the original 32,000 contracted laborers, about 6,700 stayed on to work as "dukawallas," the artisans, traders, clerks, and, finally, small administrators. Excluded from colonial government and farming, they straddled the middle economic ground above the native blacks. Some even became doctors and lawyers.

Despite animosity from native Africans and restrictions by colonial whites, Africa still provided more opportunities than crowded, caste-rigid colonial India. East Africa became America for Indians in the first half of the 20th century, and their resourcefulness cannot be understated or discounted.

It was the dukawalla, not white settlers, who first moved into new colonial areas, laying the groundwork for the colonialist economy based on cash for food and goods. And even before the dukawallas, Indian traders had followed the Arab trading routes inland on the coast of modern-day Kenya and Tanzania. Indians had a virtual lock on Zanzibar's lucrative trade in the 19th century, working as the Sultan's exclusive agents.

Between the building of the railways and the end of World War II, the number of Indians in East Africa swelled to 320,000.

By the 1940s, some colonial areas had already passed laws restricting the flow of immigrants, as did white-ruled

Rhodesia in 1924. But by then, the Indians had firmly established control of commercial trade - some 80 to 90 percent in Kenya and Uganda - plus sections of industrial development. In 1948, all but 12 of Uganda's 195 cotton ginneries were Indian-run.

The lives of the Mhindi (Swahili for Indian) were first fictionalized for a Western mass audience in V.S. Naipul's *A Bend in the River*. The West Indies author's 1979 book remains the best-known literary work in English addressing the Indian experience in East and Central Africa.

Though recently *A Bend* enjoyed a resurgence of critical acclaim for its dead-on portrayal of post-colonial African life in the former Zaire (renamed the Democratic Republic of Congo), the novel also lifted the curtain on an ethnic group who had become central to East Africa's life in the later half of the 20th century.

A Bend concerns Salim, a Moslem Indian shopkeeper born in an unnamed East African country (presumably Tanzania) who opens a small shop in another unnamed country (Zaire), in an unnamed river town (Kisangani), during the late 1960s.

Salim is Naipul's everyman dukawalla, trading in bric-a-brac, making a profit by turning, as Naipul says, two into four.

In Salim's words, his store "had bolts of cloth and oilcloth on the shelves, but most of the stock was spread out on the concrete floor. I sat on a desk in the middle of my concrete barn, facing the door, with a concrete pillar next to the desk give me some feeling of being anchored in that sea of junk... ."

With clarity, Naipul details Salim's precarious life under ex-Zairian dictator Mobutu Sese Seko. In Salim's narrative, Naipul also brings to life the African Indians, the widely scattered commercial class you still see in every East African city, many running shops that today are more upscale than Salim's.

A Bend also portrays the more successful dukawalla, Nazruddin, Salim's benefactor who moves from Zaire, to Uganda, to London, to Canada, and back to London again.

Though the book was published 18 years ago, Naipul's Nazruddin closely resembles many modern-day entrepreneurs sitting around me on the jumbo jet, with their family investments in Africa and abroad: "He still had interests in his old country - a shop, a few agencies," writes Naipul of Nazruddin. "He had thought it prudent to keep the shop on, while he was transferring his assets out of the country, to prevent people looking at his affairs too closely."

Faced with the nationalization of all "foreign" businesses by "the big man," Salim ultimately leaves the town by the river. Though Naipul never says it, it's presumed the once-and-future trader will join Nazruddin again in England and marry Kareisha, Nazruddin's daughter. That union, Naipul makes clear, is as much a business deal as it is a family one.

Family is also at the heart of the 1991 film "Mississippi Masala." Directed by Indian-born Mira Nair, the story concerns a Ugandan Indian family living in Mississippi whose adult daughter (Sarita Choudhury) becomes romantically involved with a Southern black man (Denzel Washington).

The relationship potentially threatens to undo the family's ethnic solidarity and its economic vitality. The affair also ignites old racial fears of the woman's father, who experiences flashbacks to his Uganda youth and his family's sudden and violent exile in August 1972.

At that time, Uganda's then-infamous dictator, Idi Amin, gave the nearly 75,000 Ugandans of Asian descent 90 days to pack their bags and leave the country. These descendants of the dukawallas and Indian coolies then comprised about 2 percent of the population.

In Uganda I talked with numerous Ugandan-born Indians who said their families left with just "the shirt on

218

their backs." Their businesses were "Africanized" and given to Amin's cohorts, only to be plundered and ruined. The country lost a valuable class of professionals, sliding into a chaos that would eventually claim up to 750,000 Ugandan lives.

Some 27,000 Ugandan Indians moved to Britain, another 6,100 to Canada, 1,100 to the United States, while the rest scattered to other Asian and European countries.

Today, however, many of these same ethnic Indians have returned.

In 1992, under pressure from aid donors and Western governments, Ugandan President Yoweri Museveni simplified a then 10-year-old law letting Asians reacquire lost property.

While many black Ugandans have learned the art of business during their Asian brethren's absence, Indians today still run many shops, hotels, and factories in Kampala, the capital, as do ethnic Indians in Kenyan and Tanzanian cities.

Temples, such as the Sikh and Hindu temples in Kampala, figure prominently in the urban East African urban landscape. And some extended families - the backbone of the Indian ethnic group - are prospering under Uganda's new openness. Two extended Indian families, the Mehtas and Madhvanis, have built multimillion dollar empires in Uganda since the 1980s.

The average visitor to Uganda will likely meet prosperous Indians just about anywhere. My companion on the Entebbe flight, an Indian woman from London whose parents were born in Uganda, was met at the Entebbe airport by her cousin, whose family drove a new Toyota sedan. She told me they were planning a safari holiday for her.

A day later I saw a new 1997 Mercedes Benz coup with Uganda plates driven by two Indian men at the Rwandan border. According to the Ugandan border policemen who knew them, they were returning to

Kampala after a business trip to research starting a factory in Kigali.

An elderly man with glasses, a large facial wart, and a cigarette forever dangling from his lips, Ravish, is not pretty. The retired Canadian civil servant from Toronto, however, is prosperous, as a tour of his modest hotel apartment showed.

He took pride pointing to his new appliances: refrigerator, stove, television, stereo. His youthful days long gone, Ravish was entering his twilight years as a comfortable African businessman, firmly straddling his Canadian and Ugandan worlds.

Looking out from the third-story terrace of his hotel over the 40,000-person city of Mbale, in eastern Uganda, Ravish describes the town of his birth. "Mbale used to be the cleanest city in East Africa," said Ravish, who returned in 1996 to reclaim his downtown properties seized during the Amin years. "Now look at it."

A commercial center at the base of the 4,300-meter dormant volcano Mt. Elgon, Mbale is filled with concrete buildings dating from the 1930s. They wear an Asian architectural style common throughout East African cities. Today, the paint is chipping on most Mbale buildings, while dark, black stains scar the crumbling concrete exteriors.

Ravish said every building in Uganda, Kenya, and what is now Tanzania used to be owned by Indian families.

Ravish said he has restored his building, which houses his hotel, shops, and a Moslem restaurant, to its former state. (It was the nicest building I saw in Mbale). He was negotiating for the return of his other downtown building in order to open a nightclub.

But difficulties had arisen, as in other cities, because the Ugandans who had seized property from their Indian neighbors had since sold their old property and now would lose everything if they left the confiscated holdings.

Like Ravish, Salim had prospered under Uganda's new

openness. I met Salim, a Canadian businessman, on the same Alliance Airlines flight that had originated in Dar es Salaam and had picked up passengers in Entebbe before heading to London. He, and primarily other ethnic Indians, had boarded in Entebbe.

Salim said he spent the last year in Kampala helping run his family's mercantile business. Born in Dar es Salaam, Salim now holds a navy-blue Canadian passport and calls Vancouver, British Columbia, home. In British Columbia, his family runs two hotels and was thinking about opening a nursing home. Good profits and a stable investment, he said.

Uganda, however, was more risky, despite its free-market capitalism and successful debt repayments that led the IMF and the World Bank to cancel Uganda's outstanding debt to foreign donors in April.

In Salim's eyes, Uganda's one-party rule by the National Resistance Council was not so open or business friendly. He said excessive value-added tariffs made some business ventures impossible. Even regular Ugandans despised government taxation, despite the government's efforts to ease some restrictions.

A mob attack in Mbale against the Ugandan Revenue Authority in mid-June left three officials wounded by machetes, provoking a police crackdown the following week. I saw roadblocks up on all exits and well-armed police making morning sweeps of the local bus station days after the anti-taxation violence.

A young, mustached man in his 30s, interested exclusively in business, Salim said Indian families in Uganda believed the country's current calm could change overnight. "All it would take is one bullet in Museveni's head," he said.

Ugandan Indian families he knows all have emergency plans ready. They have provisions and currency hidden for such a disaster. Those with dual citizenship are registered with the Canadian embassy, he said. "All they need is a plane ticket," he said. And, if necessary, they would leave the country overnight by vehicle.

Salim described this unease matter-of-factly. He made it sound like an entire business class, a pillar in the East African economy, is prepared for economic and political chaos.

Continued fighting in western Uganda between hundreds of rebels and troops in June and politically motivated ethnic violence in Mombasa, Kenya, that claimed more than 40 lives in August gave credence to these concerns.

But the Indians I met would survive. They had learned their lessons under Amin. They would prevail through proven institutions: strong families and marriage alliances kept within the Indian circle.

You see that in the large Indian families walking the streets together in Dar es Salaam, in Arusha, in Kampala, the woman dressed in elegant saris or salvaar kameez, children in hand.

In the event of chaos, they would join existing family operations in the New World, in Canada, and even the U.S. Meanwhile, they would comfortably continue straddling both hemispheres.

I shook Salim's hand goodbye at the baggage-claim carousel of Vancouver's international airport. It was a cold grip, not a warm, three-part African handshake extended by many black African men and women I had met in Uganda, Kenya, and Tanzania.

As an African, Salim knew the meaning of this shorter shake, and knew that I did I too. He was a businessman, and I was not a part of a business deal requiring a meaningful grasp.

Watching Salim walk off to meet his business partner, his father, I recalled my conversation with Shabir. He said Indians from Africa or Canada or the United Kingdom could never relate to Indians from India.

I believed him, that the ethnic Indians from Africa

could not mix with native Indians. I believed him that Indian caste traditions led tens of thousands of Indians to originally leave their homeland and settle in East Africa be reborn as a business class. I was less sure African Indians had shed their "Indian-ness" during their diaspora in Africa.

When I returned to Seattle, I called a retired minister friend who had lived a quarter century in Tamil Nadu, India.

He had never spent time in Africa, though his long ship voyages from India that passed by Africa were filled with Indian businessmen owning African investments. When I described the number of Indians I had met on my recent journey, he laughed outright. "Indians, ohhh," he said, "they're the best businessmen in the world."

Appendix III:

The Swahili People and The Swahili Culture

THE Swahili are found mostly in Kenya and Tanzania along the coast. They are also found in urban centres in other parts of both countries but not in large numbers as they are in the coastal regions. And they are mostly Muslim.

The contrast is sometimes glaring. For example, when I was growing up in Rungwe District in the Southern Highlands of Tanganyika, later Tanzania, there was not a single mosque in the town of Tukuyu, the district headquarters, or in the entire district. And there were very few Muslims, only a handful, mostly in Tukuyu.

But it was an entirely different story along the coast and in many other urban centres in the country.

Although the Swahili people, or Waswahili as they are known in the Kiswahili language, are considered to be de-tribalised Africans, members of tribes indigenous to the coast are also considered to be Waswahili.

One of the best examples are the Zaramo, or Wazaramo, in Tanzania who are the original inhabitants of

Dar es Salaam (formerly known as Mzizima when it was a village), the former capital which is now the commercial centre although in most cases it is still the capital city of Tanzania. Even the president of Tanzania still lives in Dar es Salaam, not in Dodoma, in the hinterland, which is the official capital.

The Swahili have lived along the coast for centuries, probably since 100 A.D.

There were African tribes along the coast, and when the Arabs came, they interacted and intermarried with the indigenous people. The product of this intermingling was the Swahili people and Swahili culture.

Therefore most of the people who are called Swahili or Waswahili are a mixed group of people, racially with the Arabs, and in terms of inter-tribal marriage of coastal tribes who were from the beginning strongly influenced by the Arabs and adopted Islam and Arab culture.

Persians, especially in what is Tanzania today, also contributed to the evolution of the Swahili people and the Swahili culture. They came mostly from a region called Shiraz in Persia, now Iran, and their descendants who intermarried with Africans still live in Zanzibar today. They are also found in other parts of Tanzania and even in Kenya.

But marriage between Arabs and Africans, and between Persians and Africans, was one-sided in the sense that it was Arab men and Persian men who married black African women or kept them as concubines. It was unthinkable for African men to marry Arab women or Persian women. And the intermarriage was mostly between Arabs and Africans. Persians who settled in East Africa were far fewer than the Arabs who migrated to the region through the centuries.

What is also important to remember is that there was no Islam before the prophet Mohammed. Yet there were Arabs who settled in East Africa long before Islam became a religion, and long before Mohammed was born.

Therefore evolution of Swahili culture - a product of intermingling and intermarriage between Arabs and Africans - started long before the advent and propagation of Islam. But it was reinforced centuries later with the spread of the Islamic faith. And the Swahili people themselves came into being before Islam since racial intermarriage between Arabs and Africans started taking place centuries before Islam became a religion.

It was not until the 700s A.D. that Islam was introduced to East Africa after prophet Mohammed died in 632 A.D. It was also during that period that Arabs started settling in East Africa in large numbers, many of them spreading the Islamic faith.

But while Swahilisation of the East African coast and evolution of the Swahili culture preceded Islam, Islam did, centuries later especially since the 700s A.D., profoundly influence Swahili culture and in fact virtually transformed it into Islamic culture, clearly demonstrated even today on the East African coast where almost all the Swahili people are Muslims, or Moslems, whichever term they prefer to use.

What is also important to remember is that it was not just those who were the product of inter-racial marriage between Arabs and Africans who became or were considered to be Swahili people together with de-tribalised Africans and tribal Africans who had adopted Swahili culture. Arabs themselves also became Swahili, or Waswahili, just like their black counterparts and those of mixed race.

Even today, Arabs in Kenya and Tanzania are called - and consider themselves to be - Waswahili. The Swahili identity transcends race.

Most of the Arabs in Kenya and Tanzania speak Swahili, or Kiswahili, as their mother-tongue although they are also bilingual and speak Arabic as well.

Even many Swahili people who have African and Arab ancestry also speak Arabic although Kiswahili is their

226

native language as much as it is for de-tribalised black Africans who don't know their tribal languages.

Tanzania has more people whose mother-tongue is Kiswahili than Kenya does. But Kenya also has some Waswahili, especially those in Mombasa and Lamu, who are more "typical Swahili" than many Swahili people in Tanzania.

One of them is renowned Kenyan scholar, Professor Ali Mazrui from Mombasa, who is both black African and Arab in terms of racial heritage, as many people along the East African coast are. As he has emphatically stated on a number of occasions, Kiswahili is his mother-tongue, or his native language. But he also speaks Arabic. And he is a Muslm.

He is a typical Swahili – in spite of being Westernised in terms of education and lifestyle – and has the following to say about the Swahili people and the Swahili culture in one of his lectures:

Uswahili International:
Between Language and Cultural Synthesis

Professor Ali A. Mazrui

Delivered at Fort Jesus, Mombasa, Kenya, on 19 July 2005, as part of the launch of the Swahili Resource Centre, Coastal Branch, Kenya.

The event was also a commemoration of the works of Sheikh Al-Amin Ali Mazrui, the late Chief Kadhi of Kenya who was also the father of the future professor, Ali Amin Mazrui, who was 14 years old when his father died in 1947 at the age of 58.

This Resource Centre is primarily focused on Swahili culture, rather than the Swahili language.

Is there a Swahili culture apart from the language? A

culture is a way of life of a people.

In order for there to be a distinct Swahili culture, there has to be a distinct Swahili people. Is there a Swahili people with a distinct way of life of its own?

The Swahili people are those who originated the Swahili language. They themselves emerged at the Coast of Kenya and Tanzania; they were originally overwhelmingly Muslim and they had strong cultural links with Coastal African tribes, on the one hand, and the Arabian peninsular, on the other.

Like medieval Islam, Swahili culture was enhanced by a spirit of *creative synthesis*. Islamic civilization was at its best when it was prepared to learn from other cultures and civilizations.

In mathematics ancient Islamic civilization was stimulated by India. In philosophy Islamic civilization was stimulated by ancient Greeks. In architecture Islamic civilization was stimulated by pre-Islamic Persia. In asylum and political refuge early Muslims enjoyed the protection of Africans in the Horn of Africa.

During the lifetime of the Prophet Muhammad himself, Arab Muslims were being persecuted by pre-Islamic Arabs on the Arabian peninsular. A group of endangered Arab Muslims crossed the Red Sea into Abyssinia (now called Ethiopia) in search of political asylum and religious refuge.

They were protected by an African Christian monarch. Among the refugees was Uthman bin Affan, later destined to become the third Caliph of Islam and the protector of the Qur'an.

Islamic civilization subsequently declined when it became less and less ready to learn from other civilizations, and condemned major cultural changes as bid'a - that is, as dangerous innovations.

Like ancient Islamic civilization, Swahili culture initially prospered through a spirit of *creative synthesis* – ready to learn from other cultures.

While the basic foundation of the Kiswahili language was Bantu African, the language quite early demonstrated readiness to borrow extensively from Arabic.

Sometimes the configuration of Arabic and Bantu African concepts constituted a remarkable balancing act.

Bantu:
Kusini na Kaskazini – North and South
Arabic:
Mashariki na Magharibi – East and West
Bantu:
Uchumi – Economics
Arabic:
Siasa – Politics
Bantu:
Bunge – Parliament
Arabic:
Raisi – President
Bantu:
Balozi – Ambassador
Arabic:
Waziri – Minister
Bantu:
Chumvi (or Munyu) – Salt
Arabic:
Sukari – Sugar
Bantu:
Mungu – God
Arabic:
Angel – Malaika
Bantu:
Nguvu – Strength
Arabic:
Afya – Health
Bantu:
Utumwa – Slavery
Arabic:

Uhuru – Freedom
Bantu:
Mjomba – Maternal Uncle
Arabic:
Ami – Paternal Uncle
Bantu:
Shangazi – Paternal Aunt
Arabic:
Khalati – Maternal Aunt
Bantu:
Nyama – Meat
Arabic:
Samaki – Fish
Bantu:
Mto – River
Arabic:
Bahari – Ocean or Sea
Bantu:
Moja, Mbili, Tatu. Nne, Tano – One, Two, Three, Four, Five
Arabic:
Sita, Saba, Tisa – Six, Seven, Nine
Bantu:
Kumi – Ten
Arabic:
Ishirini mpaka Mia – Twenty to a Hundred

In interacting with both Arab and Indian civilizations, Swahili architecture and systems of decoration were affected.

Elaborately carved Lamu doors, copper decorated chests, ivory decorated Lamu thrones, entered Swahili decorative worlds – as well as beautiful copper coffee pots and the small coffee cups.

In the creative synthesis Swahili culture helped to Africanize the tabla (Indian drum) for events which have ranged from tarabu (Swahili concert) to maulidi (celebrating the Prophet's birthday), alongside matari (dancing drums with small bells attached).

Arabic music also provided the ud to Swahili culture – an Arabian Nights guitar.

The Swahili flute was influenced by both Middle Eastern and South Asian orchestration.

Creative synthesis also incorporated into Kiswahili several food cuisines. Swahili cuisine seeks to incorporate such South Asian dishes as pilau, biriani, and chapatti – none of which are identical with the Indian varieties.

Some of the spices carry Arab names rather than Indian – such as bizari for curry powder and thumu or thomo for garlic.

Swahili architecture in places like Lamu and the ruins of Gedi continue to reflect this responsiveness to the cultures of other societies.

This Fort Jesus was built by the Portuguese. It was from time to time Swahilized, especially when the rulers of Mombasa were for a while either Swahilized Arabs or Arabized Waswahili.

The Portuguese brought maize to East Africa. Most Europeans at the time called maize "Indian corn".

The word "Indian" refers to Americo-Indians (Red Indians, rather than Hindustan).

To the present day, the name for maize in Kiswahili is hindi (singular) or mahindi (plural). A salute to Montezuma, the Emperor of Mexico.

Words we have borrowed from Portuguese include the big one – pesa, meaning money. It is borrowed from pesos, the Iberian currency.

Other Portuguese words: sapatu (slippers), shimizi (female undergarment), kandirinya (water kettle).

The Germans gave Kiswahili such educational words as shule (school). The Arabs gave us elimu (scholarly knowledge), the Africans gave us chuo and chuo kikuu (educational institution and university), and the British gave us words which range from profesa to sayansi, from baiskeli to dimokrasi, and from manuwari (man of war – or battleship) to sinema (cinema).

This readiness to respond to other cultures and languages makes Kiswahili very similar to the English language. Both languages have been spectacularly successful. English words which the British have borrowed from Arabic include algebra, tariff (from taarifa), admiral (from emir), and, surprisingly, alcohol (al-quhl).

The most famous English loan word borrowed from Kiswahili is the word safari. In English the word means "hunting trip in Africa" – though in Swahili usage safari refers to any kind of travelling.

Kiswahili borrowed the word from Arabic and then loaned the word to the English language. *Creative synthesis* in all its intricate interconnections.

We must conclude that although the Swahili language is the legacy of words, the Swahili culture is a much wider phenomenon – including marriage customs, the traditions of child rearing, cuisine, architecture, dress code.

Kiswahili has greatly influenced neighboring African languages. The kanzu in Kenya is associated with Swahili culture, and most wearers of the kanzu in Kenya are Muslims.

The kanzu in Uganda is not associated with any religion. The Kabaka of Buganda – a leading member of the Anglican global community – often wears the kanzu on ceremonial Christian occasions.

The word for religion in Luganda is dini. "Dini" also serves the same purpose in a large number of other East African indigenous languages.

Today we start an enterprise about Swahili culture as a whole. We have also honored Sheikh Al-Amin Aly Mazrui because he was one of the most influential writers of the Swahili language and a major expert of the manners, customs and beliefs of the Waswahili.

May this enterprise be blessed by our ancestors,

supported by our people, served by our community, protected by our government and helped to grow to full maturity and triumph by the Almighty God. Amen.

Kila tunapomsheherekea mtu mwema, huwa na sisi tuna wema ndani ya nyoyo zetu.

An American playwright [John Drinkwater] has captured the same spirit in the following words about Abraham Lincoln:

When the high heart we magnify,
And the sure vision celebrate,
And worship greatness passing by,
Ourselves are great.

On a day like this I am proud and grateful that my father's high heart has been magnified, his sure vision celebrated, and his greatness suitably recognized.

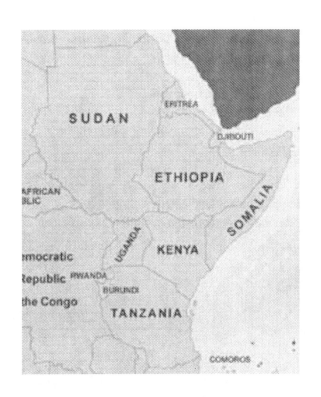

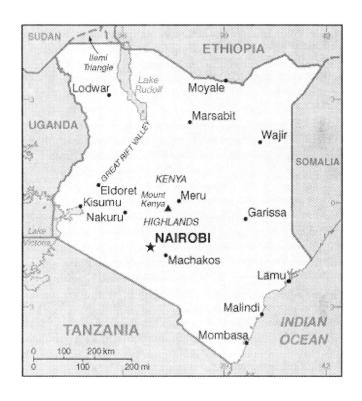

235

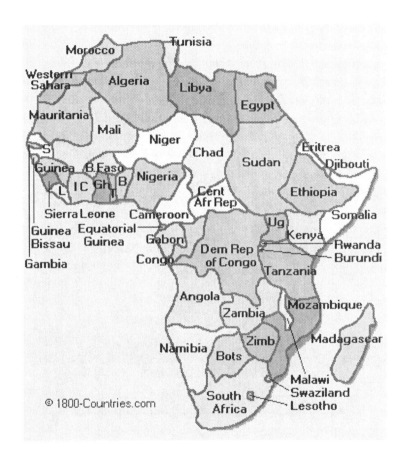

Printed in the United States
209968BV00004B/12/A

9 780980 258790